DIALOGUE

Dialogue is a many-sided critical concept; at once an ancient philosophical genre, a formal component of fiction and drama, a model for the relationship of writer and reader, and a theoretical key to the nature of language. In all its forms, it questions 'literature', disturbing the singleness and fixity of the written text with the fluid interactivity of conversation.

In this clear and concise guide to the multiple significance of the term, Peter Womack:

- outlines the history of dialogue form, looking at Platonic, Renaissance, Enlightenment and Modern examples;
- illustrates the play of dialogue in the many 'voices' of the novel, and considers how dialogue works on the stage;
- interprets the influential dialogic theories of Mikhail Bakhtin;
- examines the idea that literary study itself consists of a 'dialogue' with the past;
- presents a useful glossary and further reading section.

Practical and thought-provoking, this volume is the ideal starting-point for the exploration of this diverse and fascinating literary form.

Peter Womack is Professor of Literature and Drama at the University of East Anglia.

THE NEW CRITICAL IDIOM

SERIES EDITOR: JOHN DRAKAKIS, UNIVERSITY OF STIRLING

The New Critical Idiom is an invaluable series of introductory guides to today's critical terminology. Each book:

- provides a handy, explanatory guide to the use (and abuse) of the term;
- offers an original and distinctive overview by a leading literary and cultural critic;
- relates the term to the larger field of cultural representation.

With a strong emphasis on clarity, lively debate and the widest possible breadth of examples, *The New Critical Idiom* is an indispensable approach to key topics in literary studies.

Also available in this series:

DIALOGUE

Peter Womack

Routledge
Taylor & Francis Group

LONDON AND NEW YORK

First published 2011
by Routledge
2 Park Square, Milton Park, Abingdon, OX14 4RN

Simultaneously published in the USA and Canada
by Routledge
711 Third Avenue, New York, NY 10017

Routledge is an imprint of the Taylor & Francis Group, an informa business

Typeset in Garamond and Scala Sans by Tayor & Francis Books

British Library Cataloguing in Publication Data
A catalogue record for this book is available from the British Library

Library of Congress Cataloging in Publication Data
Womack, Peter, 1952-
    Dialogue / Peter Womack. – 1st ed.
      p. cm. – (The New critical idiom)
    Includes bibliographical references and index.
    1. Dialogue analysis. I. Title.
    P95.455.W63 2010
    401'.43 – dc22
            2010046804

ISBN: 978-0-415-32921-7 (hbk)
ISBN: 978-0-415-32922-4 (pbk)
ISBN: 978-0-203-39127-3 (ebk)

MIX
Paper from
responsible sources
FSC
www.fsc.org FSC® C004839

Printed and bound in Great Britain by
TJ International Ltd, Padstow, Cornwall

For Laura

CONTENTS

ACKNOWLEDGEMENTS

I wrote this book because I am not very good at dialogue. So it is a particular pleasure to note how deeply it has benefited from conversations with friends and colleagues. Many thanks to my skilful interlocutors, especially Jon Cook, Mark Currie, Tony Gash, Denise Riley, Victor Sage and Laura Scott. I am also indebted, like all the authors in this series, to the editorial vigilance of John Drakakis.

ABBREVIATIONS

The books by Bakhtin that I have quoted most often, *The Dialogic Imagination* and *Problems of Dostoevsky's Poetics*, are cited in the text as *DI* and *PDP* respectively.

SERIES EDITOR'S PREFACE

The New Critical Idiom is a series of introductory books which seeks to extend the lexicon of literary terms, in order to address the radical changes which have taken place in the study of literature during the last decades of the twentieth century. The aim is to provide clear, well-illustrated accounts of the full range of terminology currently in use, and to evolve histories of its changing usage.

The current state of the discipline of literary studies is one where there is considerable debate concerning basic questions of terminology. This involves, among other things, the boundaries which distinguish the literary from the non-literary; the position of literature within the larger sphere of culture; the relationship between literatures of different cultures; and questions concerning the relation of literary to other cultural forms within the context of interdisciplinary studies.

It is clear that the field of literary criticism and theory is a dynamic and heterogeneous one. The present need is for individual volumes on terms which combine clarity of exposition with an adventurousness of perspective and a breadth of application. Each volume will contain as part of its apparatus some indication of the direction in which the definition of particular terms is likely to move, as well as expanding the disciplinary boundaries within which some of these terms have been traditionally contained. This will involve some re-situation of terms within the larger field of cultural representation, and will introduce examples from the area of film and the modern media in addition to examples from a variety of literary texts.

INTRODUCTION

In one of his essays, the strange and brilliant German writer Heinrich von Kleist (1777–1811) reflects on a famous incident that took place at the beginning of the French Revolution. On 23 June 1789, as the political crisis deepened, the Comte de Mirabeau declared that the Estates-General, the elected assembly of France, would not disperse unless compelled to do so by bayonets. This spirited assertion of the rights of the people rang round Europe and made Mirabeau a hero. Kleist, writing less than 20 years later, offers his own reconstruction of the way the celebrated words came to be spoken. The king had ordered the dissolution of the Estates, and the royal officer, seeing that the delegates were still seated in the chamber, re-entered to ask them whether they had heard the king's command.

> 'Yes,' Mirabeau replied, 'we have heard the King's command.' – I am certain that beginning thus humanely he had not yet thought of the bayonets with which he would finish. 'Yes, my dear sir,' he repeated, 'we have heard it.' – As we see, he is not yet exactly sure what he intends. 'But by what right ... ' he continues, and suddenly a source of colossal ideas is opened up to him, 'do you give us orders here? We

are the representatives of the nation.' – That was what he needed! – 'The nation does not take orders. It gives them.' – Which launches him there and then to the highest pitch of boldness. – 'And to make myself perfectly plain to you ... ' – And only now does he find words to express how fully his soul has armed itself and stands ready to resist – 'Tell your king we shall not move from here unless forced to by bayonets.' – Whereupon, well content with himself, he sat down.

(Kleist 1997: 406)

As Kleist tells it, this is a story about the virtue of talking. The words with which Mirabeau made history were not the formulation of a principle that was ready and waiting in his mind. Rather, the royal officer's question made it necessary for him to say something, and then what he said gave him the idea of saying something else, and so on until he arrived at his magnificent conclusion. That is to say, the relation between the thought and the speech was not, as you might suppose, that the speech was the medium of the thought, but that the thought was the product of the speech. Adapting the French proverb, *'l'appétit vient en mangeant'* (appetite comes with eating), Kleist suggests that *'l'idée vient en parlant'* (the idea comes with speaking). It was *en parlant* – while speaking and through the process of speaking – that Mirabeau discovered the intellectual and political boldness the situation demanded. He was the man of the moment because he had talked himself into it.

This suggestion turns out to be surprisingly subversive. If it can be generalised, it implies that our ideas are not so much the legitimate creation of our minds as the by-product of our interactions. It is when I am animated by the act of talking to someone that my soul, or my tongue, or something in between the two, is impelled to invent. My idea arises not from my contemplation of the world, but from the fact that, having started, I have to get to the end somehow, and I am both stimulated by the implications of my last sentence and under pressure to come up with my next one. Look for instance at the moment when Mirabeau says 'We are the representatives of the nation', and Kleist comments, 'That was what he needed!' He hears Mirabeau's sentence not simply as something he said, but also as something he happened to find, like a person scrabbling around in a moment of danger and luckily putting his hand on a weapon. *Now* he knows what his next move is. This theory has the effect of displacing individual consciousness from the throne it conventionally occupies: it imagines thought not as a thing inside somebody's mind, but as an activity that goes on *between* people. One can no more think alone than play tennis alone; there has to be another player returning the ball. In short, it suggests that our mental life is rooted not in ourselves, but in dialogue.

This proposition makes the concept of dialogue crucial to our understanding of language, of meaning, and of literature. But it also raises an immediate and obvious difficulty. If it is true that thought is a function of speech, and speech a function of the interaction between people, then surely it follows that, as the German philosopher Hans-Georg Gadamer puts it in a book to which we will return in the final chapter, 'language is by nature the language of conversation' (Gadamer 2004: 443). Language lives on people's lips as they fill it with their active, social presence; locked up in a book, abstracted from the activity of speaking and answering and reduced to a silent code, it is almost literally a shadow of its former self. So if we say that dialogue is central to the life of language, it seems we have to add at once that writing is, by definition, alienated from it. Literature appears, precisely, as the attempt to play tennis by oneself. Books don't talk, so how can they be part of a dialogue?

Alhough that has the air of a rhetorical question, it does not seem to me to be unanswerable. In fact, the rest of this book is essentially devoted to trying to answer it. One possible answer is that writing is fascinated and formed by dialogue *because* it is in a literal sense the thing it cannot be. Rather in the way that sculpture is in love with movement, literature is drawn to the unattainable immediacy of speech; dialogue is the intensely apprehended thing that lives just beyond the limits of the written. Kleist's story illustrates this in its minute attention to the movement of Mirabeau's spoken words: a sort of breathless commentary follows him phrase by phrase, tracing each successive nuance with a specificity that would be impossible in real time. 'Language is by nature the language of conversation', but artificial language can articulate an awareness of that nature that is unavailable to conversation itself. Talk in literature is imaginatively radiant because of its literal absence.

That could be called a dialectical answer to the question about writing and dialogue: it takes it for granted that speech is the opposite of writing, that dialogue belongs to speech, and consequently that when writing endeavours to construct or encompass dialogue, it is confronting its own negation. This is an illuminating answer to pursue because the binary opposition in which it is based is so deeply and widely shared. In effect, it is a trope that runs all the way through Western thought, from its announcement in Plato's *Phaedrus* to its deconstruction in Derrida's *Of Grammatology*. Orality and literacy, breath and calligraphy, the transient presence of utterance versus the abstract permanence of script: this fraught pairing reappears whenever writing undertakes to represent speech.

The four chapters of this book, then, represent four ways in which writing has sought to engage in dialogue despite its own inability to talk. The first chapter gives an account of dialogue as a literary genre: that is, the kind of philosophical essay which, following Plato, takes the form of an oral discussion supposedly remembered and transcribed. Here, in a tradition going back almost to the beginnings of European literacy, writing engages with speech by means of falsification: the literary text *pretends* to be the record of a conversation. The second chapter concentrates on the novel, crucially and almost universally a literary form that has dialogue *in it*. To describe imaginary people talking to each other, and to present the reader with what purport to be their actual words, is one of the defining procedures of the genre. In other words, novels characteristically *represent* conversations, an operation which we shall see is stranger and more complicated than its familiarity makes it seem. The third chapter is about drama. This is in a way writing's most frontal and obvious attempt to escape from its own silence: the writer puts words in the mouths of physical speakers who really do talk, deploying a sophisticated technique to disguise the writtenness of the lines and make them sound like unpremeditated utterances. In other words, this is a form that *simulates* conversation. The fourth chapter shifts to the question of how literature is understood, exploring the possibilities and complications of the idea that interpretation, especially the interpretation of texts from the past, can most accurately be imagined as, itself, a form of dialogue. In this last case, writing adopts conversation as a *metaphor*.

But all this does not exhaust the question 'How can books be part of a dialogue when they don't talk?' Writers of dialogue are doing more than just aspiring to the immediacy of speech, or consoling themselves for their inability to attain it. If we return to Kleist's story, for example, we can see that it does not merely describe a dialogue, it also *constitutes* one. The dialogue it describes is the one between Mirabeau and the royal officer; the dialogue it constitutes is the one between Mirabeau and Kleist. The paragraph I quoted is structured by the rapid alternations between these two speakers: we hear Mirabeau's voice, then Kleist's interjecting, almost interrrupting, then Mirabeau continuing, and so on. A dash occurs nine times, and it becomes clear that Kleist is using it to mark the point at which the word passes from one speaker to the other; but even this improvised punctuation is not quite able to keep up with the agility of the back-and-forth movement. We hear the two voices as a dialogue, not only because of the speed and neatness of the switching, but also because they refract one another as we read. The grandeur of Mirabeau's declaration is slightly skewed by the ironic effect of Kleist's interjections, but at the same time, you can hear Kleist's prose identifying with Mirabeau, as the narrative begins and ends in the past tense, but in the middle is drawn into the excitable present tense of live commentary. What is striking about this secondary dialogue is that it is inherently and necessarily literary. The intersecting of the two speakers' words is neither presented nor imaginable as a literal conversation; they meet *only* on the page, only as narrator and hero within the medium of a written story. Here, then, is an example of writing which does not copy or transcribe dialogue from a spoken original but, on the contrary, creates its own. This distinctively written kind of dialogue is an object of interest throughout this book: in other words, we will investigate not only the sense in which writing cannot possibly be dialogue, but also the sense in which it can be and is.

Writing which *is* dialogue is often called 'dialogic', or 'dialogical'. These words come fairly directly from the English translations of the Russian thinker and critic Mikhail Bakhtin, who placed the concept of dialogue at the very centre of his work. His influence is such that, today, any theoretical book about dialogue is bound in part to be a book about Bakhtinian 'dialogism'. However, I have tried not to let this almost unpronounceable neologism, with its air of technical specialism, become disconnected from the word in general use. The meaning Bakhtin attaches to 'dialogue' is not quite the same as its everyday meaning; but it is not altogether different either. It is through thinking about dialogue in the ordinary senses of the word that we work out what the concept of 'the dialogic' implies, and what use it might be. Consequently, Bakhtin features in this book frequently but irregularly: I will be concerned with some forms of dialogue that he did not recognise as well as some that he did, and also with the connections between them.

Since this means that my understanding of 'dialogue' is going to be eclectic, I should perhaps pre-empt one connotation that is currently quite strong: the association of dialogue with the values of liberal politics. Dialogue is good because everyone's point of view is valid in its own way, and the truest and wisest conclusions are reached through a discussion in which everyone gets a fair crack of the whip. Government and people, management and workforce, Protestants and Catholics, should speak and listen to one another, because the alternatives to dialogue are arbitrary authority and violent conflict. Dialogue is the discursive form of democracy, because it means talking to someone in the expectation that they will talk back on the same basis, thus positing a formal equality between speaker and addressee. These arguments and principles are by no means irrelevant to the subject of this book: as Chapters 1 and 2 will both make clear in different contexts, a powerful tradition links dialogue form to the idea of freedom of speech, to the secular exercise of reason in the face of religious authority, and to the power of laughter to disrupt the closures of official pronouncements. In short, dialogue is historically aligned with political liberty. It is hardly an accident that Kleist's little fable is, itself, about a felicitous refusal to obey an arbitrary order.

All the same, this inclusive and co-operative ideal of dialogue is clearly not what Kleist, at least, has in mind. The speech in the story does not take the form of a balanced exchange of views; after the initial question, only Mirabeau says anything at all. The royal officer is vividly present as the *addressee* of his speech: first answered, then questioned, and finally instructed, he is essential to the performance. But nobody is interested in his views; his only importance is that he constitutes the situation that elicits Mirabeau's words. That is to say: the idea of dialogue does not in itself carry a promise of parity in the relations between interlocutors. They may be equal, in status and in the amount they say, but they may be grossly unequal. They may learn from one another in a mutual fashion, but it is equally possible that one just teaches and the other just learns, so that the teacher learns nothing new. Or one participant may be no more than a sounding board for the other's ideas. There is a tendency for moralistic and managerial champions of dialogue to regard such assymmetries as a sort of disqualification: if, for example, it is an article of faith that 'In a dialogue, everybody wins', then a dialogue in which somebody loses is not really a dialogue at all (Bohm 2004: 7). But there is no warrant for this value-laden restriction of the term. Dialogue is the interaction of distinct speakers, and there is no guarantee that the interaction will not turn out to be authoritarian, or slanted, or deceitful, or lacking in respect. What I am interested in is not the metaphysical separation of 'true' and 'false' dialogue, but the unpredictable semantic energy generated by the interaction itself.

1

THE GENRE

'Whoever philosophises, simulates a dialogue.'
Konrad Lorenz (Mittelstrass 1988: 128)

The default verb for essay questions in the humanities is 'discuss'. 'Discuss Shakespeare's uses of disguise'; '"The First World War was entirely avoidable." Discuss.' Because this imperative is so familiar, we tend not to notice that it is also contradictory. As an examination candidate, I am required on the one hand to produce a discussion, that is, an exchange of views, a conversation with others. But on the other hand, I am forbidden to exchange a single word with the people around me. Moreover, the purpose of the prohibition is to make sure that what I ultimately hand in will be my own unaided work, uncontaminated by the contribution of anyone else. Thus what I am supposed to be doing is described as a dialogue, but the circumstances in which I am to do it are vigilantly monologic.

This equivocation is not confined to the examination hall. Classic works in the humanities, especially in philosophy, often describe themselves as 'enquiring' or 'investigating'. The eighteenth-century writer Edmund Burke made his reputation with *A*

Philosophical Enquiry into the Origin of our Ideas of the Sublime and the Beautiful. Karl Marx announces on the first page of *Capital*: 'Our investigation therefore begins with the analysis of the commodity.' Ludwig Wittgenstein's most influential book is entitled *Philosophical Investigations.* These ways of putting it suggest a speaker who is asking questions, listening to answers, formulating further questions, engaging in the back-and-forth interactions with others that take up the time of real-life enquirers and investigators. But in fact, once again, the texts turn out to be the uninterrupted discourses of their authors. The promise of dialogue is not to be taken literally; it is a false prospectus, or a metaphor, or something in between.

So as we work in history, or philosophy, or the social sciences, or the study of literature and the arts, we find that our writing is as it were haunted by the idea of dialogue. The lecturers' lectures are distracted and enlivened by a feeling that they ought to be, or would like to be, conversations. This resonant absence is felt most of all in the dialogue *genre*, that form of philosophical exposition that goes so far as to invent imaginary characters and write out their supposed exchanges complete with speech headings, so that the text looks rather like the script of a play. Normally, a dialogue of this kind purports to be the transcript of an actual conversation, as if the represented philosophers had been chatting away in the company of a shorthand reporter. But only the most unsophisticated reader believes this: rather, the differentiated speakers are understood to be a literary device, a way of writing an essay so that it really does appear to 'enquire', to 'investigate', and to 'discuss'.

The dialogue in this sense is very old indeed. It is the form of almost all the works of Plato (427–347 BCE), and is in that sense the *original* method of writing philosophy in the West. Plato wrote some two dozen dialogues, most of them presented as records of the teaching of his mentor Socrates (469–399 BCE). Socrates himself wrote nothing; he is shown going about Athens asking people hard questions, challenging their metaphysical and ethical assumptions, and teaching students in ones and twos by an intensive method of question and answer. He therefore appears as the person who actually did the questioning and investigating which writers only say they do. Understandably, then, Platonic dialogue has had a secular prestige and influence. It is imitated, for instance, in Cicero's writings on rhetoric and metaphysics (55–45 BCE), in Thomas More's *Utopia* (1516), in Galileo's demolition of the geocentric cosmos (1632), in George Berkeley's *Three Dialogues* (1713). The history of European thought cannot be done without dialogues. Yet despite this cultural grandeur, there is also something about the genre that is obscure, marginal, almost whimsical. Nobody anthologises or teaches it like 'tragedy' or 'the novel'. Some dialogues do deal with classical philosophical issues, such as the nature of language or the existence of God, but many deal with much more limited topics, like archery, or English policy in Ireland, or whether the Elizabethan age was better or worse than the eighteenth century. Many of the more recent examples come from a distinctive and intriguing class of epistemological troublemakers: David Hume, Denis Diderot, the Marquis de Sade, Heinrich von Kleist, Thomas Love Peacock, Oscar Wilde, Edward Gordon Craig. One slightly surprising recent English exponent was Vivienne Westwood, who in 2008 produced a wide-ranging cultural 'Manifesto' in fantastical dialogue form. The genre was appropriate, both to the oddity of her decision, and to the half-serious subversiveness that has characterised her career in fashion. Despite its originary status, dialogue seems typically to be the preferred medium of eccentrics and provocateurs.

This chapter traces the possibilities of this paradoxical genre by taking five canonical dialogues, from the ancient world, the Renaissance, the Enlightenment, and the very edge of modernity, and exploring their particular structures in order to arrive at a general understanding of what is at stake. Since the genre works differently at different cultural moments, the formal account has also to be, in the same breath, an outline history.

PLATONIC DIALOGUE: PLATO, *PHAEDRUS*

Plato's *Phaedrus* was written between 375 and 365 BCE, and the conversation it presents is supposed to have taken place about 50 years earlier. Socrates, out walking, meets his friend Phaedrus, who has just been with a fashionable orator called Lysias, and has brought away a copy of his new speech. They make themselves comfortable beside a stream, and Phaedrus reads the speech aloud. It comes out of the pederastic culture of its time and place, when it was conventional for mature men to adopt adolescent boys as both intellectual protegés and physical lovers, and it argues that a boy is better advised to grant his favours to a man who does not love him than to one who does. Phaedrus thinks this speech very clever, but Socrates disagrees, and makes his point by improvising a cleverer one to the same effect. Then, suddenly ashamed of this game of denigrating love, he makes an even better speech in its praise. In the aftermath of this trio of speeches, the friends discuss rhetoric itself, asking whether it is an art, and what the conditions of excellence in it are. This exploration leads to a famous final section in which Socrates argues that writing is a trivial and careless use of words, and that the only serious communicative medium is conversation; so the dialogue concludes with an implicit reflection on its own form.

For our purposes the conclusion is crucial: why is writing inferior to talk? According to Socrates, a man who possesses knowledge communicates it by planting it in the soil of a receptive soul. Since he is doing something important and difficult, he is careful to choose an appropriate recipient, to speak to that person in a way which is suited to his nature, to confirm by questioning him that he has understood, and to deal with his perplexities by inviting him to ask questions in his turn. Only through this painstaking process, which Socrates calls dialectic, will the transplanted knowledge take root and live. By these standards, writing a book is an act of shocking indifference to the fate of one's thought. Written discourse has no idea who it is addressing; it says the same thing to everybody whether it is appropriate or not; and although it may appear articulate and intelligent, if anyone questions what it says it is unable to reply. It can neither accommodate itself to its friends nor defend itself against its enemies, but wanders around the world useless and helpless (Plato 1995: 274c–278e). Thus writing is condemned by comparison not with speech in general, but specifically with interactive speech, that is to say, with dialogue. What the text *represents* becomes the occasion of a devastating critique of what it *is*.

This paradox points us towards the heart of dialogue as a literary form. After all, the point is not just that writing and conversation are different. It is that (as Socrates argues it) the opposition between them is constitutive: conversation, in its responsiveness, its adaptability, its interpersonal life, defines exactly what writing is not. By mimicking conversation, then, the written text latches onto its own structural opposite; this is writing trying to escape its own essential condition. That is of course impossible. But what is the effect of trying?

Most obviously, it is to embed the philosophical ideas in a fictional situation. For example, in Socrates' great speech about the trans-formative power of love, he assures us that the human soul can acquire wings. He goes into some detail about these wings: when and how they grow, in what circumstances they are damaged or fall away, what kinds of nourishment make them stronger, and so on, all in a rather insanely bland and informative tone (246c–251e). If all this were being advanced by Plato as a metaphysical system, it would be so odd that it would be difficult to take it seriously. But that is not what is happening. Rather, this is supposed to be a speech improvised by Socrates for a number of definite purposes: it is to persuade the hypothetical boy not to be taken in by the dubious arguments of Lysias, it is to take away the bad taste of the false oratory that has just been heard, it is to pacify the God of Love with a speech in his praise, it is to entertain Socrates' friend Phaedrus, who likes this sort of thing. More inwardly, it is also pedagogic: since previous speeches have denigrated love by calling it a kind of madness, this one questions the assumption that madness is always bad, and prompts the listener to imagine a visionary madness, a delusion which is the perception of a higher reality. In other words, the wings are not a doctrine; rather, they are explicitly offered as one way of putting something. On another day, with a less offensive starting point or a less quick-witted interlocutor, it would be put quite differently. Dialogue, then, has the effect of making the exposition provisional, pragmatic, context-dependent.

This is not to imply, in some general-purpose gesture of scepticism, that all knowledge is relative. On the contrary, the assumption that there *is* such a thing as absolute truth is the basis of the whole form. Truth, for Plato, is permanent, unchanging and noncontradictory, whereas human speech is transient, inconstant and ambiguous. Consequently, every attempt to put the truth into words is a failure of one kind or another. The great merit of the dialogue form, from this point of view, is that it wears its inadequacy on its sleeve. Socrates and Phaedrus meet by chance; their discussion is casual and improvisatory; both of them change their minds as it proceeds; any conclusions they come to are rendered uncertain by Socrates' characteristic irony; it is obvious that the whole encounter is partly fictional anyway. All these signs work together not to minimise the unreliability of language but positively to advertise it. Unlike Lysias' written oration, with its deceptive air of covering everything, Plato's discourse is conspicuously local and partial. The truth about love, or language, is not situated in these words, but born in the minds of the interlocutors; the text reaches out beyond its own limits for a completion it evidently fails to contain in itself.

So the dialogue paradoxically pursues stable truth by means of unstable words. Or, to put it another way, dialogue form foregrounds philosophical processes rather than philosophical propositions. Philosophy, on this interpretation, is primarily a way of living; knowledge is vouchsafed not to those who adopt the right doctrines, but to those who undertake the right exercises, so that their minds acquire the strength and accuracy to apprehend real things (Mittelstrass 1988). Written dialogue constitutes a sort of pattern book for this practice: it shows the mental activity that is required, the patience, cunning, friendliness and daring of truly philosophic conversation. But it is only a pattern book; you cannot learn philosophy by reading about it, any more than you can learn to cook by reading recipes; to make real progress you must begin to do it. On this view, Platonic dialogue is *exemplary*, saying not so much 'This is the truth' as 'This is the kind of thing you need to do in order to arrive at the truth.'

It is therefore a matter of substance, not just of presentational charm, that the *Phaedrus* is a kind of idyll. Socrates and Phaedrus leave the city in the heat of the day, and talk under a flowering plane tree with their feet in a cool spring. Socrates plays half-seriously with the idea that the spring is sacred to the Nymphs, and that they are invisibly inspiring his eloquence. The whole conversation, then, is a retreat, a pleasant suspension of normal business. This bracketing is especially poignant in the historical retrospect which is part of Plato's context. Phaedrus was exiled by the Athenian state in 415 BCE, and Socrates himself was put to death in 399 BCE for allegedly corrupting the city's youth. The dialogue commemorates two victims of official suppression by imagining them in a situation where they speak freely and without fear. The image proved influential. For example, *De Oratore*, Cicero's treatise on rhetoric, written about 300 years later, takes the form of a discussion at a politician's country house. A bruising political confrontation is in progress in Rome, and a group of friends have left the city for a few days' break. There is a plane tree in the grounds, so they decide to imitate the *Phaedrus* by settling down in its shade, forgetting the immediate crisis, and instead holding a philosophical discussion of oratory (Cicero 1942: i, vii, 28–30). Like Plato's, the dialogue was not written until several decades after it supposedly took place, and in the meantime many of the participants had met their deaths in the lethal politics of the late Roman Republic. Again, then, the dialogue itself is idyllic, almost utopian: *here*, in contrast to the follies and brutalities of the city, is the right way to seek wisdom, in ease, sociability, and good faith. The exposition of the ideas is, in the same breath, the evocation of a good way to live.

But how does this affect the argument? A short extract from the *Phaedrus* will suggest an answer. This is from the sequence that directly analyses the art of speaking. Socrates has just attacked rhetoric as a technique for representing things as good irrespective of their actual merit, a system of words divorced from real knowledge. Then he pulls back for a moment:

SOCRATES: But could it be, my friend, that we have mocked the art of speaking more rudely than it deserves? For it might perhaps reply, 'What bizarre nonsense! Look, I am not forcing anyone to learn how to make speeches without knowing the truth. ... But I do make this boast: even someone who knows the truth couldn't produce conviction on the basis of a systematic art without me.'
PHAEDRUS: Well, is that a fair reply?

SOCRATES: Yes, it is – if, that is, the arguments now advancing upon rhetoric
testify that it is an art. For it seems to me that I hear certain arguments
approaching and protesting that it is a lie and that rhetoric is not an
art but an artless practice. ...

PHAEDRUS: We need to hear these arguments, Socrates. Come, produce
them, and examine them: What is their point? How do they make it?

SOCRATES: Come to us, then, noble creatures; convince Phaedrus, him of
the beautiful offspring, that unless he pursues philosophy properly he
will never be able to make a proper speech on any subject either. And
let Phaedrus be the one to answer.

PHAEDRUS: Let them put their questions.

SOCRATES: Well, then. ...

(260d–261a)

The tone is playful: Socrates teases Phaedrus by complimenting him
on his 'beautiful offspring' (he means the pretty speeches engendered
by Phaedrus' passion for rhetoric), and Phaedrus teases Socrates by
imitating his addiction to asking questions. The discursive clowning fills the discussion with imaginary voices. 'Rhetoric' indignantly
defends herself against Socrates' attack; then he hears a group of
'arguments' approaching with a fresh counter-attack on her; then, at
the end of the extract, he is preparing to put *their* questions to
Phaedrus. This subtle ventriloquism extends the principle of dialogue far beyond the two interlocutors who are supposed to be
actually present: we hear not simply what Socrates says, but what
he imagines saying to Lysias, what he would say if he *were* Lysias,
what the nymphs of the spring cause him to say, what he and
Phaedrus might say to a hypothetical defender of rhetoric. Successive
speakers are fancifully improvised and collapsed, and so the different possible positions within the argument are articulated in a
way that is both light and objective: the playfulness makes for
inventiveness, and the teasing for a sceptical lucidity. Thus the
pleasure of the conversation, as we watch Socrates and Phaedrus
enjoying themselves and each other, is neither a distraction from
the philosophical argument nor a device to make it palatable to the
reader. Rather, the enjoyment and the argument are the same thing.

It is this celebration of the pleasure of dialectic that forms the
Phaedrus's strongest link between its conclusion (Socrates' attack

on writing) and its apparently remote starting point (Lysias' attack on love). Lysias' speech is the only written text within the dialogue, and its fate exemplifies the delusions of writing: initially impressive, it is exposed to increasingly destructive criticism as the discussion develops, because its parent Lysias is not there to look after it, and it has no power to stick up for itself. This neglect on his part is consistent with the nature of the speech itself, which is a rhetorical showpiece, aiming, as Socrates argues, not at what is true, but at what is convincing. Its manner is bright, plausible, uncommitted; we are to suppose that Lysias could argue just as effectively on the other side of the case. He cares as little about the truth or falsehood of his speech as he does about what happens to it. That is consistent, in turn, with the proposition he is advancing, namely, that a dispassionate suitor is to be preferred to one who is in love, because lovers are distracted and unreliable, whereas with a non-lover it is possible to come to a reasonable, mutually advantageous arrangement. So every level of Lysias's speech is characterised by the same uncommitted efficiency: this is the utterance of somebody who doesn't love the boy, doesn't love the truth, and doesn't love the offspring of his own mind. Socrates, on the other hand, speaks as a lover. His second speech is formally dedicated to Eros; the wisdom it contains is embedded both in the speaker's courtship of the hypothetical boy who is the addressee of all the speeches and in Socrates' affec-tionate, flirtatious relationship with Phaedrus; the whole loquacious afternoon is, itself, an instance of the devotion with which he plants his seed in the soil of a congenial soul. Above all there is his love of wisdom itself. Right at the end, Socrates reflects that even the most right-thinking man should not be called 'wise', as only the gods are wise. Such a man should properly be called a lover of wisdom, that is, since the Greek words for 'love' and 'wisdom' are *philos* and *sophia*, a philosopher.

In the end, then, the *Phaedrus*, which at first appears to be a dialogue about love, and then shifts its attention to rhetoric, finally turns out to be about love after all, because only the man who speaks with love can really be described as speaking well. This unifying conception founds knowledge in relationship, in desire, in an orientation to other people or to the gods. Dialogue therefore appears as the only possible philosophical discourse, and literary dialogue as philosophy's ironic apology for entrusting itself to the loveless medium of writing.

RENAISSANCE DIALOGUE: BALDESAR CASTIGLIONE, *THE BOOK OF THE COURTIER*

In a way, then, Socratic dialogue is writing that distrusts writing. As classical Rome received it from Athens, and the European Renaissance received it from Rome, it drew further away from its authentically oral origins, and established itself as a literary form. But it still implied an ambivalent attitude to its own literariness, remaining open to the contention that writing is a poor vehicle for conveying knowledge.

This proposition is likely to be resisted by modern readers, not only because they are readers, but also because they are modern. After all, writing has been the decisive medium of modernity itself: the Reformation, the nation state, Enlightenment, industrialisation, mass education, and liberal politics are all unimaginable without the more or less unrestricted circulation of the written word. Writing is ideologically and practically linked with beliefs that most readers of a book like this one take for granted: that it is good to communicate one's knowledge to as many people as possible, that freedom of information and expression are basic human rights, that secrecy is always an evil, though ocasionally a necessary one. To suggest that human beings would learn more if writing had not been invented contravenes not only our daily practice but also our faith in open communications. To privilege face-to-face conversation instead is to propose an *esoteric* model for the passing on of knowledge: that is, one in which the truth is revealed not to all and sundry, but to those who are judged capable of it (Szlezák 1999). Teaching becomes less a matter of dissemination, more a matter of initiation.

That opposition, which is given in very general terms by the bare existence of writing, was posited much more specifically, from the mid fifteenth century on, by the invention of printing. Fairly suddenly, the readership of a text became both larger and more anonymous: the word was not restricted to those deemed fit to receive it (on whatever grounds of faith or rank or learning), but offered indifferently to anyone who could read, or who knew someone who could. Print tends to undo the social and cultural differentiation of the addressee, and was in that sense at odds with the extremely hierarchical institutions that formed the main sites of early modern culture: churches, courts, universities. It is perhaps not surprising, then, that hundreds of early modern books were composed in dialogue form. The convention was used for a great range of subjects, from learned satire to popular religious instruction, and from farm management to national politics. It is as if the abstracting and levelling character of print could be attenuated by the pretence that the book was a conversation: through a sort of textual fiction, the speaker reconstructed the distinction that publication threatened to efface.

This tricky negotiation between coterie and public is virtuosically conducted in Castiglione's *The Book of the Courtier*. A treatise in dialogue form, it was first published in 1528 and became one of the most influential books of the European Renaissance, reprinted, translated, and cited throughout the next two centuries (Burke 1995). The conversation it records is supposed to have taken place in 1507, in the central Italian dukedom of Urbino. An illustrious group of courtiers, assembled for a papal visit, decide to prolong the festivities after the Pope's departure by a conversational game: between them they will fashion the image of a perfect courtier. Their conversation eventually extends over four evenings, each with a different leading speaker: the first of these expounds the perfect courtier's qualities, the second develops the manner in which he should put these qualities to use, the third corrects the male bias of the first two by discussing the qualities to be looked for in a female courtier, and the last extends the terms of the discussion by asking about the 'end' of the perfect courtier (that is, the courtier's *raison d'être*, the larger purposes he or she serves).

It would be something of an understatement, then, to describe Castiglione's book as 'elitist'. It describes a dozen or so individuals, selected by social and cultural criteria that exclude almost everybody, engaging for their own amusement in brilliant but lightweight conversation about the minutiae of their lives: how should a courtier dress? what variety of Italian should he speak?

what should he do if his prince requires him to do something dishonourable? In the whole of sixteenth-century Europe there are only a few hundred people to whom these questions are of direct concern. It is possible that the book will have a wider circulation than that; but the book is in any case presented as a secondary product, a mere amanuensis scribbling down an account of what was said so that the memory of such eloquence should not be altogether lost. In the preface, the author apologises for placing so trifling a sketch before his noble dedicatee (Castiglione 1967: 31–32). The communicative space that matters is not the book, but the charmed circle at Urbino, which the reader will never enter.

On the other hand the book is not like that at all. It is, both by design and in effect, the manifesto of a powerful secular ideal of civility, composed and published for the world and for posterity. The ideal is worked out in the universal terms of ethics, politics, aesthetics and, in the sublime conclusion of the fourth night, sexual love. In short, a complete conception of what it is to be human is at stake. Castiglione's disclaimers about the book are themselves a piece of courtiership; he spent years polishing its style, and ensured that physically it was the most magnificent object the Venetian printing industry could produce. The 'trifling sketch' is his life's work. He even makes it clear that when the original conversations took place in 1507 he himself was away in England, which means that he is not the amanuensis after all, but the author. So far from humbly commemorating its fine ladies and gentlemen, the text imperiously employs them as its *dramatis personae*. The communicative space that matters is not a game played by a few courtiers 20 years before, but the volume in the reader's hands.

A published dialogue, in other words, is both a conversation and a printed text: as the first, it belongs to a coterie, and as the second, it belongs to a public. It thus allows Castiglione to commit himself to both spheres at once, and to negotiate the tension between them. We can see the negotiation in detail by taking almost any passage to examine more closely. Towards the end of the second evening, the conversation turns to the question of jokes: how, and within what limits of taste, will our perfect courtier make us laugh? The speaker who carries this topic, Bernardo, develops it with an unnecessary wealth of examples; he is not only discussing the courtier's duty to amuse but at the same time discharging it. At the end he adds that one's repertoire of pleasantries should not include anything that impugns the honour of women (195). This is an appropriate conclusion for him to reach, because the whole conversation takes place in the presence of the Duchess of Urbino, who has delegated her authority to her principal lady in waiting: Bernardo is rounding off his discourse with a polite bow to those who charged him to make it in the first place. However, the group also contains some anti-feminists, one of whom, Gaspare, questions this conclusion: why should women's honour be any more protected from mockery than men's? Bernardo's reply is that men themselves made the rule that a lapse in a man's virtue is overlooked, but a lapse in a woman's virtue disgraces her for ever, from which it follows that women's reputations need to be respected more vigilantly than men's. A third speaker, named Ottaviano, adds that Gaspare could defend this alleged rule by appealing to the general frailty and weakness of women: since they are incapable of most of the virtues for which we admire men, it is necessary to impose upon them a simple, negative rule which it is possible for them to keep. The exchange seems to be developing into a broad battle-of-the-sexes debate, and Bernardo mischievously suggests that since none of the ladies present has objected to Gaspare and Ottaviano's slighting remarks, they must be right in assuming that women do not mind what bad things are said about them so long as their chastity is not impugned. The ladies, thus provoked, run laughingly at Gaspare and rain mock-blows upon him with their fans, an exercise which dispels the drowsiness that had begun to affect the company, since the hour is getting late (195–200).

What *kind* of discourse does this typical sequence display? Most striking, perhaps, is its capacity to tack between seriousness and frivolity. A minor question of etiquette, in itself little more than a pretext for telling some jokes, mutates into a major question of moral philosophy: is virtue in men and women the same thing or two different things? Then, without being fully resolved, it is dissipated in a moment of graceful clowning. This fluidity of attitude is itself one of the ideal courtier's virtues: he must be able, as Bernardo is here, to enforce important truths without becoming unsociably didactic. This is at bottom a political issue. If the courtier cannot carry a serious point, he will fail to gain influence over the prince; but if he advances his argument too seriously, he will be challenging the prince's authority, and so will lose his influence through his unseemly arrogance. He must contrive to have it both ways: to exercise power submissively, to speak instructively and pleasantly in the same breath. This subtle skill is exemplified not only by many of Castiglione's characters, but also by the conception of his book as a whole, a philosophical search for perfection which never ceases also to be a description of an upper-class diversion.

The exchanges are game-like not only because they avoid earnestness, but also because they are rule-governed. When Gaspare objects to Bernardo's privileging of women's honour, he is challenging him to produce a logical reason why it is not just arbitrary. Bernardo adduces the double standard governing sexual misconduct: *that*, he implies, is the arbitrary distinction, and his own is merely a corollary of it. But then Ottaviano's intervention seeks to represent the double standard itself as logical by grounding it in the distinct natures of men and women. And so on. These people are not just swapping their opinions. In order to maintain a position within the debate, a speaker must acknowledge its consequences, defend it against objections, ensure that no-one is offended by it: in short, he must accept a rule of accountability for what he says. Indicatively, Ottaviano explains that his theory of women's inferiority is not his own view but merely an argument that Gaspare could use. That may be true, or it may just be a way of avoiding being rude to the Duchess: either way, it speaks a discursive world in which arguments are not the expression of anyone's inner convictions so much as strategies to be used instrumentally and as it were neutrally, like moves in a game.

The intellectual context that makes the game possible can be named in one word: rhetoric. It is not only that *The Courtier* is explicitly indebted to Cicero's classic rhetorical textbook *De Oratore*; and not only that Castiglione's speakers have a continued and detailed interest in questions of language and style. It is also that they have a shared conception of speech as performative. Rhetoric is, after all – as formulated in classical Greece and Rome, and revived in the academies of the Renaissance – a systematic training not just in speech but in speech *acts*. It is designed to teach people how to use words effectively to congratulate, accuse, mollify, prove, belittle, thank, intimidate, divert. The intention is always to do something; the utterance does not describe an action, it *is* one. In *The Courtier*, accordingly, speaking is never just a neutral vehicle for conveying ideas or information; it is also, perhaps primarily, a piece of behaviour. Thus, for example, when Bernardo makes his speech about the double standard, it would be a mistake to conclude that he is an early feminist. Rather, what he is doing is negating, as forcefully as he can, Gaspare's contention that male and female honour are entitled to equal respect. And he is doing that for two reasons: first, that Gaspare is attacking what he just said, and it would be feeble of him not to defend his position; and second, that having found himself in the role of advocate for the Duchess and her ladies, he is obliged by his honour to do the best for them that he can. Similarly, when, a few moments later, he teasingly accuses the same ladies of caring only about their reputation for chastity and ignoring every other virtue, it is not because he has suddenly turned into an anti-feminist. Rather, it is because he has noticed that the confrontation with Gaspare is on the edge of becoming both discourteous and irrelevant; his little provocation averts this danger both by turning the conversation back towards jocularity and by inviting the ladies to rejoin it. Being good at talking in this sense is rather like being good at dancing: alertness, agility, and a sharp sense of the appropriate are at least as important as the content of what you say.

That is not to imply that *The Book of the Courtier* is indifferent to the truth of the ideas it puts forward. The point is rather that, operating within the intensely pragmatic verbal and conceptual system of rhetoric, it takes the truth about '*cortesia*' to be situational, a matter, as Castiglione points out, of custom and usage, not of pure reason (39–40). The difference between a praiseworthy speech and a despicable one, between a formulation which does its author honour and one of which he should be ashamed, is not a free-standing or universal principle, but is tied up with who is speaking, and to whom, and for what purposes, though the praise and contempt and honour and shame are no less decisive for that. In other words, the truth is immersed in the social situation whose truth it is, and that is why it cannot without misrepresentation be abstracted from the rule-governed conversations in which it develops and lives. However many thousands of readers the book acquires, it still needs for its validity the conversation in which it is founded.

On the other hand, that indebtedness is reciprocal. The conversation also needs the book because, as we saw, its poised, interactive perfection is the outcome of years of *literary* labour: the origin of the writing in speech is one that the writing has constructed for itself. Dialogue is talk in highly idealised form, so it cannot simply represent the side of conversation against writing, aristocratic presence against the abstraction of print. Rather, it is an expression of the relationship between the two.

ENLIGHTENMENT DIALOGUE: DAVID HUME, *DIALOGUES CONCERNING NATURAL RELIGION*, AND GALILEO GALILEI, *DIALOGUE CONCERNING THE TWO CHIEF WORLD SYSTEMS*

For a century and more after the publication of *The Book of the Courtier*, dialogue form was a commonplace way of composing essays and treatises. The home of the genre was Italy, but it also flourished in most European languages, certainly including English. Some dialogues are widely read today for reasons unconnected with their form: for example Philip Stubbes, *Anatomie of Abuses* (1583), Edmund Spenser, *A View of the Present State of Ireland* (written in 1596), or John Dryden, *Of Dramatic Poetry: An Essay* (1668). These stand for dozens of less well-known contemporaries. The writers of these texts do not necessarily have any great interest in the formal possibilities of dialogue. Rather, they use it as an off-the-peg instrument for the exposition of information or opinion. Both Stubbes and Spenser, typically, set up a two-handed conversation between an expert and a person who wishes to be better informed. The latter is a transparent proxy for the reader within what substantially remains a monologic text: the dialogue works rather like the FAQs section of a modern website. In short, the genre was a recognised and useful medium for communicating knowledge. Certainly it offered special opportunities for irony, ambiguity and open-endedness, and Dryden, for example, gracefully exploits some of them. But dialogue was also, all along, just one way in which a writer with no special literary pretensions might choose to present his material.

By the time of our next stopping point in the history of dialogue, this ready availability has gone. The *Dialogues Concerning Natural Religion,* by the sceptical philosopher David Hume (1711–76), were written in the 1750s and published posthumously in 1779. By this time, as Hume acknowledges in a preface, dialogue was no longer accepted as a generally valid form of exposition. Modern philosophy, he says, is expected to consist of 'accurate and regular argument', and therefore to proceed methodically, like a mathematical demonstration, not in the indirect and improvisatory style of a conversation (Hume 1976: 143). This admission prompts two questions at once. Why had dialogue ceased to seem a reliable intellectual vehicle? And why did Hume choose it all the same? The answers to both questions are connected to his intellectual environment.

Hume's Edinburgh was one of the two capitals of the eighteenth-century Enlightenment, the other, greater one being the Paris of Voltaire, Diderot, and Rousseau. Like most important cultural events, 'the Enlightenment' was named only in historical retrospect; but even at the time, both cities contained circles of writers and intellectuals who were conscious of forming a new movement, with shared principles and shared enemies. Perhaps the most important of the principles was that truth is grounded in experience, so that what we know is what we perceive, or is the result of reasoning on the basis of what we perceive; and much of what we think we know, not being based on experience, is not knowledge at all, but prejudice, or metaphysical speculation, or blind faith. The heroes of the Enlightenment were consequently natural scientists, above all the seventeenth-century mathematician and physicist Isaac Newton.

This emphasis suggests why Hume thinks dialogue is passé. If the decisive components of knowledge are observation and reasoning, then language has value only as a medium for transmitting the observations and reasons accurately from one person to another. Stylistically, this function demands neutrality rather than eloquence: words represent things, and should confine themselves to not distorting them. The rhetorical framework of Renaissance dialogue therefore loses its rationale; and this was in fact the historical point at which the term 'rhetoric' began its decline towards its dismissive modern sense of 'empty words'. So the intense interest in verbal performance which we saw in Castiglione evaporates: constructing the exposition of one's idea as an interchange of speeches merely wastes words and distracts from the essential content. Moreover, the purpose of this set of intellectual virtues (accuracy, regularity, reasoning from experience) is to arrive at conclusions which are as far as possible certain: that is, which establish features of the world that remain the same whoever is looking at them, and propositions which remain true whoever is enunciating them. If this is achieved, the particular context of utterance is neither here nor there, and so the fictional framework of dialogue becomes pointless.

In this idea that truth consists of contextless, universal propositions, there is a sort of belated retort to the attack on writing in the *Phaedrus*. If what is required of an utterance is accuracy, then what Socrates identified as the weaknesses of writing are transformed into strengths. He had complained that a written statement is incapable of change: it says the same thing to everyone however inappropriate, and never responds to questions. But this incapacity can be reread as integrity: written records are not influenced by irrelevant circumstances, they don't tell one story today and a different one tomorrow. Now, writing appears as the most reliable vehicle of knowledge, exactly because it is impersonal, ascertainable, immune to the imprecision and inconsistency that bedevil the spoken word. It is not an accident that the Enlightenment, though carried forward by some intensely convivial individuals, defined itself above all by producing an encyclopedia. If classical dialogue form is the sign of an admission of secondariness, an assumption that written text is a more or less inadequate simulation of real (i.e. spoken) communication, then this is the moment when dialogue loses its *raison d'être*. Writing stops apologising and stands on its own feet.

On the other hand, that positive account of Enlightenment is vitally incomplete. If its heroes were scientists, it also had villains, and on the whole these were religious figures: monks, inquisitors, fanatics. This adversarial way of putting it is not misleading. Both Paris and Edinburgh were characterised not only by enlightened salons but also by conservative religious establishments: France was governed by an absolute monarchy ideologically inseparable from the Roman Catholic Church, and Edinburgh was the capital city of an entrenched biblical protestantism. The Enlightenment typically defined itself against these establishments. Not that it was necessarily atheistic – on the whole it was not – but that in seeking to understand reality by observation and reason, it increasingly wanted access to questions which had previously been under religious control, such as the origin of the world, the foundations of morality, or the nature of the human soul. In other words, 'Enlightenment' does not simply mean scientific method; it means scientific method as it confronts a religious authority that has not yet ceased to be dominant. This is the context in which Hume's eccentric choice of literary form starts to make sense.

'Natural religion' is the conviction that God can be known, independently of scriptural or miraculous revelation, by the same mechanisms of perception and reasoning by which we know other things. It is true that God cannot be directly perceived, but neither can, say, gravitation, and yet the existence of gravitation is a rational conclusion to draw from our experience of the world: the claim of natural religion is that to believe in God is rational in a similar way. Its importance was that it promised to bring Enlightenment and religion into a single discourse and dissolve the opposition between them. The *Dialogues* sabotage this emollient project. They consist of a conversation in which Cleanthes, the exponent of natural religion, confronts two opponents: Demea, a Christian believer who opposes any attempt to bring the mystery of God within the limiting terms of human reason; and Philo, a philosopher who attacks Cleanthes' arguments on the grounds of their internal incoherence. The conclusion of the work assigns the victory to Cleanthes, but this does little to repair the damage that has been inflicted on his position by the sustained two-pronged interrogation. The effect of the argument as a whole is to disturb the peaceful co-existence of Christianity and natural philosophy.

Dialogues Concerning Natural Religion is thus a deliberate venture into dangerous territory. Having composed it and shown it to friends, Hume kept it in manuscript for the rest of his life, but sought to ensure that it was printed after his death. Realising that his literary executors were reluctant to take the risk, he assured them that 'nothing can be more cautiously and more artfully written', which implies that the purpose of the 'art' is to help keep the book out of trouble. No longer convincing as a medium of knowledge, dialogue acquires a different function as a tactic of evasion. By assigning heterodox views to a fictional speaker, the author can articulate them as vigorously as he likes while prudently keeping open the possibility that he does not hold them himself. The model for this defensive conception of the form, reverently mentioned by Philo, is the *Dialogue Concerning the Two Chief World Systems*, fatefully published in 1632 by Galileo Galilei. This text, situated literally on the boundary between two world views, is in that sense the foundational modern dialogue.

The two world systems are, in essence, the old Aristotelian one, according to which the earth is stationary and the sun goes round it, and the new Copernican one, according to which the earth is one of the planets orbiting the sun. The Roman Catholic Church specifically decreed that the Copernican view was contrary to Holy Scripture and therefore could not be taught, defended, or held, and it was this prohibition that led Galileo into dialogue form (Finocchiaro 1989, 147–53). Like Hume after him, he invented three interlocutors: Salviati is a Copernican mathematician, Sagredo an open-minded man of general culture, and Simplicio a fundamentalist Aristotelian. The outcome of the discussion is never in doubt: Salviati is master of the subject, Sagredo is his friend, pressing questions and objections only in order to elicit clarifications, and Simplicio is defeated at every turn. Galileo is not constructing an aporetic suspension between his two systems: he is sure that the official view is unsustainable and the prohibited view substantially correct. Rather, the form functions as a disclaimer. Galileo is not, himself, teaching, defending, or holding the heretical view of the solar system; he is merely imagining a discussion of it. Salviati certainly does teach, defend, and hold the heretical view, but Salviati is a fictional character who cannot be prosecuted.

As is well known, this tactic was unsuccessful: it was because of the publication of the *Dialogue* that Galileo was arrested, threatened with torture, and compelled to abjure the offending opinion. Even so, the deployment of the genre is interesting. Early in the discussion, for example, Simplicio responds to a question about motion by citing Aristotle, and Salviati retorts that this particular argument of Aristotle's is invalid because it assumes the point that is in question. Shocked, Simplicio begs that, since Aristotle is the founder of logic, Salviati should not be so disrespectful as to accuse him of an elementary logical error. Salviati replies:

> Simplicio, we are engaging in friendly discussion among ourselves in order to investigate certain truths. I shall never take it ill that you expose my errors; when I have not followed the thought of Aristotle, rebuke me freely, and I shall take it in good part.
>
> (Galilei 1962: 35)

This reply demarcates the dialogue as an enclave of intellectual freedom, in two related ways. First, the rules of propriety Simplicio is invoking (there are things one should simply not say about Aristotle) are suspended because this is merely 'friendly discussion among ourselves'. The provisional, uncommitting character of private talk licenses expressions which might be blamed in more formal contexts, or in print. Part of the pleasure and élan of conversation is, exactly, that people are not answerable for every word they say, and so are free to take ideological risks. Second, the discipline Salviati is accepting *instead* of that of public propriety is that, in dialogue, everything he says can be criticised. If he is wrong about Aristotle's argument, Simplicio only has to show him how, and he will retract his point.

In a way, this argument is as disingenuous as Galileo's doomed attempt to circumvent the papal censorship. This is not really a private discussion but a published dissertation in dialogue form: the insult to Aristotle, if that is what it is, is in reality already public. But there is something more eloquent here than a metatextual trick. If the Enlightenment is imagined (ideally) as the struggle of scientific enquiry to free itself from arbitrary authority, then dialogue, used in this way, is its formal paradigm. Whereas the Church is monologic, communicating in decrees and prescribed forms of words, dialogue, with its mobile play of questions and tentative formulations, imitates scientific method itself, which protects the truth, not by suppressing falsehood, but by encouraging its unconstrained expression so that it can be discredited in open discussion. In such a contest, as Salviati declares more than once, philosophy always wins, 'for if our conceptions prove true, new achievements will be made; if false, their rebuttal will further confirm the original doctrines' (37–38). This glowingly optimistic conception radically separates truth from authority.

Galileo's dialogue in fact appears in Hume's, not as an example of how to outflank repressive authority, but as a positive model of philosophic method. At the heart of natural religion is the so-called 'argument from design', that is, the contention that nature possesses the kind of complex intelligibility which our experience leads us to attribute to deliberate intention, so that the world is evidence of the existence of a prior mind in the same way that a house is evidence of the existence of a prior builder. Philo objects that our experience can lead us to no such conclusion, because we can have no experience of the making of worlds, which may for all we know be entirely unlike the building of houses. Cleanthes retorts that the same objection could be made to the Copernican world system, since no one has ever experienced the motion of the earth. No, Philo replies, but anyone can observe the motion of the moon and the other planets, and that is relevant experience if (though only if) these bodies resemble the earth. Exponents of the heliocentric system therefore needed to demonstrate that resemblance, and that is what they did.

> Galileo, beginning with the Moon, prov'd its Similarity in every particular to the Earth; its Density, its Distinction into solid and liquid, the

Variation of its Phases, the mutual Illuminations of the Earth and Moon, their mutual Eclipses, the Inequalities of the lunar Surface etc. After many Instances of this kind, with regard to all the Planets, Men plainly saw, that these Bodies became proper objects of Experience; and that the Similarity of their Nature enabled us to extend the same Arguments and Phænomena from one to the other.

In this cautious Proceeding of the Astronomers, you may read your own Condemnation.

(Part 2, 171–72)

Galileo's interlocutors did not simply accept that the planets were so similar to the earth that conclusions could be transferred from the one to the other: on the contrary, most people in the early seventeenth century believed that earthly and celestial substances had nothing in common at all. So Galileo patiently took them through one similarity after another, questioning their assumptions, and answering their questions, until eventually the qualitative distinction between the earth and the planets crumbled away. *That*, Philo insists with some warmth, is how advances in knowledge are really brought about.

Dialogue form appears, then, not as a medium of knowledge (which has migrated, as we saw, to treatises and systematic demonstrations), but as an instrument for *changing* what we know. Its mobile and provisional character, the margin of free play in its procedures, can be deployed not only against external censorship, but much more inwardly against the settled assumptions of a reader, who is cajoled by degrees into questioning the obvious and imagining the inconceivable. There is an example in the argumentative *coup de théâtre* which brings Hume's *Dialogues* to an end. The orthodox Demea, tiring of ingenious arguments for the existence of God, points out that people do not really base their faith on that kind of thinking. Rather:

each Man feels, in a manner, the Truth of Religion within his own Breast; and from a Consciousness of his Imbecility and Misery, rather than from any Reasoning, is led to seek Protection from that Being, on whom he and all Nature is dependent.

(Part 10, 219)

This is by no means a vacuous observation. If everyone feels the truth of religion within himself, then that is a kind of experience, and according to Hume's own (Enlightenment) principles, the common experience of mankind outweighs a great deal of clever speculation. Philo sympathetically joins in, and he and Demea spread themselves for a page or two on the subject of the brevity, uncertainty, and misery of human life, as expressed by innumerable poets and preachers. The tone of the discussion is becoming more and more unworldly, and Demea more and more comfortable with it, but then Philo swings round on Cleanthes and asks him how, in 'natural' terms, he derives a just and benevolent deity from such a panorama of suffering. Philo's question is not in itself new: it is what is often labelled 'the problem of evil'. What is startling, though, is the dialogic twist that states the problem in the *same voice* as the orthodox sense of the world as a vale of tears. The misery that impels Demea to kneel in humble adoration prompts Philo to postulate a First Cause neither good nor evil, a morally neutral God whom Demea finds so appalling that he soon finds a reason to leave the room. The sequence is a kind of intellectual comedy, but it is not just Hume amusing himself: the wit works to unsettle assumptions, to reveal opposed positions as similar and adjacent ones as incompatible. In short, Enlightenment dialogue appears here as an inherently subversive form, suited not, now, to the exposition of truth, but to the disruption of orthodoxy.

MODERN DIALOGUE: OSCAR WILDE, *THE DECAY OF LYING*

Despite the occasional high stakes, Enlightenment dialogue represents a relative withdrawal from seriousness. In the hands of Hume, or of Diderot, the genre is a vivid means of disturbing established opinions, but not of expounding positive truths on its own account. The business of knowledge has been taken away from speech and re-assigned to the written, the encyclopedic. And the dialogue genre had indeed passed out of the intellectual mainstream by the early nineteenth century. It is hard, for example, to imagine a modern physicist following Galileo's example and presenting his central findings to the world in the form of a fictional conversation.

There is a dispiriting monument to this withdrawal in the long series of *Imaginary Conversations* written between the 1820s and the 1850s by the English poet and essayist W.S. Landor (Landor 1927: vols 1–9). Once greatly admired, they are archly contrived encounters between historical figures: Socrates bumps into Aristophanes, Petrarch and Boccaccio discuss Dante, a Cavalier exchanges views with a Roundhead. For a moment they look like classical dialogues, but in practice they don't work in the same way at all, because they have no real interest in the content of the argument. They warm instead to the charm of the occasion, the display of character, and the evocation through stylistic pastiche of the 'spirit' of Imperial Rome, or Elizabethan England, or whatever it might be. In Landor, then, dialogue is expressly designated as archaic. Unhappy in his present age of steam engines and newspapers, the writer looks back to a half-imagined past of leisurely conversation in picturesque settings. That the genre is outdated is not contested: on the contrary, its outdatedness is precisely its appeal, and any relevance to the intellectual concerns of today would only diminish its antique glamour. In that sense, Landor writes the epitaph of dialogue form.

It is therefore interesting to see how, half a century later, Oscar Wilde revived the genre in a peculiar but highly focused way with two aesthetic essays in dialogue form: *The Decay of Lying* and *The Critic as Artist*, first published in 1889 and 1890. *The Decay of Lying* is dedicated to the proposition that the habit of representing things as they actually are has become dangerously widespread, and that a vigorous revival of the practice of telling lies is urgently needed. One of the two interlocutors, Vivian, has written an article to this effect, and he reads extracts from it to his friend Cyril, breaking off from time to time to expand on it, to answer objections, or to express somewhat tangential opinions on contemporary literature. The theme, comically paradoxical to begin with, deepens as it develops into the praise of art – 'the telling of beautiful untrue things' – as everywhere the superior of life and truth (Wilde 1996: 77). The fictional context lightly mimics the argument: the friends talk on a summer's afternoon in the library of a country house, and Cyril wants to go out and enjoy the beauty of nature, but Vivian thinks that nature is banal and repetitive, and insists on staying indoors until twilight has obscured its details and made it more amenable to falsification. Only then do the pair conclude their discussion and go for a walk.

Classical dialogue form is here alive and vigorous. In the interplay of writing and speech, and the light doubling of philosophical debate with homosexual flirtation, *The Decay of Lying* is a homage to the *Phaedrus*. Less deliberately, its unhesitating exposition of a paradox recalls the provocations of Enlightenment dialogue, and its idealising evocation of cultural privilege echoes *The Courtier*. Without Landor's nostalgia, Wilde displays a rich awareness of the tradition in which he is writing. So how does its modern revival come to be so cogent?

The broad answer to that question is that, this time, what I have called the outdatedness of dialogue is not sentimentalised, but turned round and made into a form of resistance. The essential proposition of the traditional dialogue had been that conversation is the best way of discovering and expressing knowledge. By the late nineteenth century, this claim was, as we have seen, no longer sustainable: a powerful set of binary oppositions (things and words, facts and feelings, work and leisure, the natural and the artificial) broke the union of truth and eloquence that had been at the centre of dialogue form, and indeed of the rhetorical tradition as a whole. Now, one was obliged to choose between them, and the effect of choosing truth at the expense of eloquence was to render speech incidental, insubstantial, merely a vehicle: hence the outdatedness of dialogue. In reviving it, then, Wilde is reversing exactly that logic: he is choosing eloquence at the expense of truth.

It is resistance, not in the sense of militant negation, but in the sense of keeping at bay, holding open. This is unusually explicit in a moment towards the end, when Vivian has just told a series of stories to show that life imitates fiction rather than the other way round:

CYRIL: The theory is certainly a very curious one, but to make it complete you must show that Nature, no less than Life, is an imitation of Art. Are you prepared to prove that?

VIVIAN: My dear fellow, I am prepared to prove anything.

CYRIL: Nature follows the landscape painter, then, and takes her effects from him?

VIVIAN: Certainly. Where, if not from the Impressionists, do we get those wonderful brown fogs that come creeping down our streets. ... ?

(68–69)

Here is the choice of eloquence over truth in practical form. Vivian accepts rules of *discourse*: in propounding a theory, one must be committed to its consequences, argue consistently, meet objections, and so on. Like Castiglione's Bernardo or Hume's Philo, he agrees to be held accountable for his argument: this is a systematic dialogue, not a casual exchange of opinions. But at the same time, he refuses rules of *evidence*: to say that his theory is implausible, or contrary to common sense, or incompatible with the known facts, is for him no objection to it whatever. The acceptance and the refusal together constitute the dialogue itself as an enclave of discursive play, an enclosed space where the authority of fact is suspended.

Interestingly from a formal point of view, the suspension entails a sort of oscillation in the register of the speeches. Vivian's prose sometimes sounds like this:

VIVIAN: 'Many a young man starts in life with a natural gift for exaggeration which, if nurtured in congenial and sympathetic surroundings, or by imitation of the best models, might grow into something really great and wonderful. But, as a rule, he comes to nothing. He either falls into careless habits of accuracy –'

CYRIL: My dear fellow!

VIVIAN: Please don't interrupt in the middle of a sentence. 'He either falls into careless habits of accuracy, or takes to frequenting the society of the aged and the well-informed.'

(51–52)

But it is equally capable of sounding like this:

VIVIAN: Art finds her own perfection within, and not outside of, herself. She is not to be judged by any external standard of resemblance. She is a veil, rather than a mirror. She has flowers that no forests know of, birds that no woodland possesses. She makes and unmakes many worlds, and can draw the moon from heaven with a scarlet thread. Hers are the 'forms more real than living man', and hers the great archetypes of which things that have existence are but unfinished copies.

(63)

The place of both these extracts in the same argument is plain enough: both celebrate the autonomy of the artistic imagination, and deplore its subordination to mere representational accuracy. But the way they work is quite distinct. The first is a comic performance. The interruption and its dismissal pick out the timing of the laugh, and the prissy moralism of the language announces itself as parody: a conventional vocabulary of disapproval is teasingly redirected against what Vivian goes on to call the morbid and unhealthy practice of telling the truth. The second extract, on the contrary, is literary. The evocation of Art as an uncanny goddess reproduces the cadence of Walter Pater's famous description of the Mona Lisa, which Wilde quoted elsewhere (Wilde 1996: 122–23); the explicit quotation is from Shelley's *Prometheus Unbound*; the concept of 'archetypes of which things that have existence are but unfinished copies' is Plato's. The comedian has given way to the scholar, and the proposition has become correspondingly less outrageous. The idea that art is an independent realm has a respectable intellectual pedigree, and only the scarlet thread saves Vivian from sounding positively conventional.

Vivian's position (and Wilde's) is thus unsettled, tacking between opposing extremes of paradox and platitude. Clearly the dialogue form is, among other things, a cover for that instability: the necessary movements in and out of solemnity can be passed off as the spontaneous ebb and flow of talk. Beyond that tactical convenience, though, the dialogue articulates the necessity itself, the reason for not coming to rest in the role either of aesthetic critic or comic provocateur. As in Hume, and in Galileo, the reason is to be found in the text's relationship with a powerful and hostile orthodoxy. There is, we have to imagine, an oppressive regime of truth, which insists on stable identity. It asks, 'What are you *really?*', and the point of the question is control. If the speaker is really a subject of knowledge, then he will have to accept the canons of probability, empirical evidence, representational accuracy and so on, and thus be definitively assimilated into the regime. If on the other hand the speaker is really a comedian, then he will have to give up the claim to be saying anything serious, and thus be definitively excluded from the regime. His only chance of evading definition is to find a way of prolonging the moment in which the question has not yet been answered. In other words, to keep talking; and for Wilde dialogue *is* that gallant and voluble procrastination.

As that way of putting it reminds us, truth did indeed reassert itself, oppressively, in the spring of 1895. The Marquess of Queensberry publicly addressed a note to 'Oscar Wilde, posing as a sodomite', and as is well known, Wilde responded with a prosecution for criminal libel. A transcript of the trial survives (Holland 2003). Queensberry's defence was justification: that is, his counsel, Edward Carson, needed to show that the statement complained of was true. Consequently, his presentation of the case was designed to establish that Wilde was as a matter of fact engaging in 'sodomitical' practices. In the cross-examination, then, we can see the question 'What are you really?' disclosing its coercive force: it is asking for self-incrimination. Carson's questioning imposes a framework of closed binary oppositions. Queensberry's phrase is factually accurate or it is not; the depravity of Dorian Gray is sodomy or it is not; Wilde had sex with *this* man, in *this* hotel, or he did not. To read the transcript is to watch the poised irresponsibility of Wilde's dialogues – their toying, their calculated impudence, their comically timed shifts of tone – progressively flattened by the reductive consistency of the criminal law. It is a sort of discursive tragedy: the playfulness of dialogue sets itself against the monologic order of fact, and proves too weak for the contest. Faced with a pile of documented evidence, Wilde lied in court and was lost.

However, this story about the defeat of the dialogic is qualified by a large and obvious irony, namely, that cross-examination is itself a dialogical form. Not only do the proceedings take the form of question and answer, but also the form is rule-governed: for example, the barrister must not say things that are not questions, and the witness must answer the questions he is asked. Moreover, the conversation is ludic in a way we can readily recognise from the rest of this chapter. Carson has a quasi-fictive role; he is arguing in order to win the game, and would be arguing the opposite if he had been briefed by the other side; his relentless concern to establish the truth of the matter is in a way a professional pretence. In other words, Wilde's adversary here could *also* claim to be an inheritor of the dialogue tradition.

For Wilde himself had missed something. In seizing, delightedly, on the playful capacity of dialogue to construct and collapse intellectual positions provisionally, he rendered it whimsical, unaccountable, innocent of every question of power. That suppressed the hardness and serious determination which are equally constitutive of the genre: the pedagogic control that Socrates exercises over the direction of the exchanges, or the inquisitorial persistence that Hume praises in Galileo. We recall that when Socrates speaks against writing, he is objecting not to its rigidity or its lack of charm, but to its ineffectuality. For him, it is only through dialogue that thought can impose and defend itself; monologue is too weak. Wilde, on the contrary, concedes just that demonstrative strength to the other side on the grounds that it is too boring to be worth contending for. As it turned out, this concession was fatally damaging. The version of dialogue that remained was beguiling but impoverished, lacking the intellectual or political force of the tradition it so intelligently honoured.

2

DIALOGUE IN THE NOVEL

INVERTED COMMAS

At the beginning of *Alice in Wonderland*, the heroine peeps at her older sister's book and finds it unappealing. It has no pictures or conversations, and '"what is the use of a book," thought Alice, "without pictures or conversations?"' (Carroll 1998: 1) The thought is gently funny because of Alice's unreflective pairing: in what way do pictures and conversations fall into the same category? Partly, it is that a peep is enough to confirm the absence of either, since both are visually distinctive on the page. But it is also that between them, pictures and conversations seem to Alice to be the things that a book can really have in it; take them away and you are left with nothing but the words. The implication, illogically but interestingly, is that the conversations in a text, like the pictures, are something *other* than the text itself.

This impression is enforced by the way English narrative writing is punctuated. Usually, the dialogue in a story is in inverted commas, or as people say, 'in quotes'. These marks identify the words they frame as originating from someone other than the writer of the rest of the text, and they are used frequently and vitally for this purpose in non-fictional writing: they are the way a journalist, or a historian, or a student writing an essay, can say, 'these words are not mine; I am quoting them from someone else'. Presumably, then, the novelist's inverted commas carry a similar message. As it happens, there is an example of both academic and fictional uses above. The words 'what is the use of a book without pictures or conversations?' are in two sets of inverted commas, one set because I am quoting the published words of Lewis Carroll, and another set because *he* is quoting the verbally formulated thought of Alice.

But putting it like that exposes an important difference between these two formally identical acts of quotation: namely, that only one of them is genuine. When my punctuation informs the reader that the words it frames are quoted, it is telling the truth: I did not compose the sentence about pictures and conversations, but copied it from a historically actual book. Lewis Carroll, on the other hand, *did* compose the sentence, and when he puts it in inverted commas he is only pretending to be quoting it from his heroine. Dialogue in a novel is in that sense *pseudo*-quotation. In a way, this is only an instance of the general truth that novels are fiction, and that the characters and their actions, including of course their utterances, have no extra-textual existence. But in that case dialogue forms a particularly pressing instance, because whereas every other aspect of the fictional world is in itself non-verbal and makes its impression on the reader by virtue of being written about, the characters' speech exists in the same medium as the novel itself, and so appears to be, not described or recounted, but directly given: here you may read the heroine's *very words*. This is perhaps the force of Alice's analogy with pictures: just as illustrations give you the feeling that rather than depending on descriptions of the characters you can actually see what they look like, so dialogue suggests to you that rather than just reading about them you can actually hear what they say.

The power of this suggestion is felt whenever a textbook sets out to explain the distinction between 'direct' and 'indirect' speech. This is a familiar topic of school English lessons: I am employing direct speech if I write '"I moved into this flat three years ago," said Brian,' and indirect speech if I write 'Brian said he had moved into his present flat three years before.' The difference between these alternatives turns on some rather complicated adjustments to the markers of person, time and place, and these are most easily rationalised by conceiving of indirect speech as a sort of paraphrase: whereas the first version gives Brian's own speech, the second is the speech of someone else, who heard what he said and now conveys the substance of it. This way of understanding the grammatical relationship makes direct speech the original and indirect speech a representation of it. Words inside inverted commas are primary (they were there first), and words outside them are secondary (they came later), and this rule of interpretation applies regardless of whether the literary context is fictional or not. Hence the miracle of suggestion: even though we know very well that Brian has no existence independent of this paragraph, since I invented him to illustrate a point, it is still almost impossible to resist the supposition that his utterance predates the text in which it appears. Thanks to inverted commas, imaginary people can have said real things.

It is important to register the magic of the inverted comma, because it is a source of great rhetorical power, as well as a great deal of literary pleasure. But it is also important not to be dazzled by it, since it implies a version of novelistic dialogue that is largely illusory. To look at its workings more sceptically, we need some examples, and I am going to take them from Henry Fielding's comic masterpiece *Tom Jones* (1749). Fielding (1707–54) used to be described as 'the father of the English novel', and it is not hard to see that *Tom Jones* belongs to the same genre as novels of the early twenty-first century. On the other hand, some of its detailed conventions are remote enough to give us a helpful critical distance.

The hero, Tom Jones, is a foundling who is adopted by the benevolent Squire Allworthy and educated alongside Allworthy's nephew Master Blifil by two ridiculous tutors called Thwackum and Square. Tom, who is imprudent but fundamentally good-hearted, gets into trouble all the time, while Blifil, who is an unscrupulous hypocrite, repeatedly secures the moral high ground. Tom emerges from one scrape with a broken arm, and the other characters react to his accident in various ways:

Mr Blifil visited his friend Jones but seldom, and never alone. This worthy young man, however, professed much regard for him, and as great concern at his misfortune; but cautiously avoided any intimacy, lest, as he frequently hinted, it might contaminate the sobriety of his own character. ... Not that he was so bitter as Thwackum; for he always expressed some hopes of Tom's reformation; 'which,' he said, 'the unparallelled goodness shewn by his uncle on this occasion, must certainly effect, in one not absolutely abandoned:' but concluded, 'if Mr Jones ever offends hereafter, I shall not be able to say a syllable in his favour.'

(Fielding 1966: 204–05)

The four principal clauses of the last sentence in this quotation execute a phased discursive movement from author to character. 'Not that he was so bitter as Thwackum' is a direct authorial comment: it does not at any level give the substance of Blifil's remarks, but is a comparative description of how he spoke. The next clause, 'for he always expressed some hopes of Tom's reformation', comes closer to indirect speech: more than the first clause, it gives an idea of what Blifil may be supposed to have said. All the same, it is a fairly remote kind of paraphrase: it is impossible to reconstruct Blifil's exact words from it, since it offers only an outline, and in any case talks about what he 'always' said, with the implication that it is not rendering a single utterance, but characterising something Blifil said on several different occasions, no doubt in slightly different ways. The clause after that is more specific: '"which," he said, "the unparallelled goodness shewn by his uncle on this occasion, must certainly effect, in one not absolutely abandoned"'. The punctuation makes this look like Blifil's 'direct speech', but things are not that straightforward. The antecedent of the initial 'which' is 'Tom's reformation', which is the narrator's phrase, so the clause is syntactically inseparable from the narrative, and therefore cannot quite be read as Blifil's autonomous discourse. And if we are to imagine Blifil's exact words, he would say *my* uncle'; 'his' is a trace of the grammatical logic of indirect speech. Then the final clause, 'but concluded, "if Mr Jones ever offends hereafter, I shall not be able to say a syllable in his favour"', arrives at full direct speech: now we are to suppose that the words in inverted commas are exactly what Blifil said on what seems to be a particular occasion.

From this virtuosic sentence we can see the way in which inverted commas are misleading. They denote an absolute binary opposition: either a phrase is in inverted commas or it is not; if it is, it belongs to the character, and if it is not, it belongs to the narrator. But what Fielding's gradations show is that dialogue in a novel is not really controlled by that kind of on–off switch. It is more like a dimmer, a continuum of values. At one end, the narrator speaks, in his own words, and the character is the mute object of his description, much as it would be if he were describing a horse or a spring morning. At the other end, we are given what purports to be the complete and exact words uttered by a character on a specified occasion. But in between, we may get a description of the character's mode of speech; a description with some illustrative examples; an evocation of the impression his speech made upon another character; a brief summary of his views; a sketch of the kind of thing he habitually says; a transcript of what he said with repetitions and expletives removed; an explanation of what he meant to say but was too agitated to express clearly. Some of these modes will appear in inverted commas as direct speech, and some will appear unmarked as indirect speech, but the distinction is not illuminating. It is difficult to say how many possible ways of producing the image of another's speech there are altogether, but the number is certainly higher than two.

Moreover, these are forms, not of separation from the narrative discourse, but of integration in it. This is literally true of the sentence of Fielding's that I quoted. Every word attributed to Blifil is embedded in the authorial syntax, which is strongly signalled by the connectives that begin each clause: 'not that … ', 'for … ', 'which … ', 'but … '. Fielding's narrative is not discreetly framing Blifil's speech, but setting it out, analysing it, drawing attention to the logical connections between its parts in a way it does not necessarily do itself. This analytic intervention does not stop at the frontier represented by the inverted commas, but appears within the supposedly direct speech. There is a usefully straightforward example of such infiltration a few pages later, in the speech of Allworthy's neighbour Mr Western, who, as his name suggests, is a stereotypical West Country hunting squire. Yet another misadventure leaves Tom covered in blood:

> 'Come, my lad,' says Western. '*D'off* thy *quoat* and wash thy *feace*: for *att* in a devilish pickle, I promise thee. Come, come, wash thyself, and *shat go huome* with me; and *we'l zee* to *vind* thee another *quoat*.'
>
> (247)

For a moment it looks to a modern reader as if the squire is audibly stressing the words that appear in italics. But that would make no sense. The italicised words are the ones whose idiom or pronunciation is distinctively Somerset, and they are being emphasised not by Western, who uses them unselfconsciously, but by Fielding, who is almost literally highlighting the rusticity of Western's speech and manners. The author's commentary is inscribed in unmistakable fashion upon the character's words. It is noticeable that Western's speeches are not always written in this way: many of them appear on the page in ordinary English. When that is so, we still suppose, if we think about it, that the words we are reading are pronounced in the squire's West Country accent: the standard written language, after all, neither dictates nor precludes any particular phonetic realisation. Fielding is not making his character inconsistent, but merely choosing when to make a point of the way he speaks and when to let it pass without special comment. Western's exact words, then, are determined not by fidelity to their illusory origin (what the squire 'actually said'), but by what Fielding is doing with him at the time.

In the sentence about Blifil, the permeation of the character's speech by authorial intention is less explicitly marked but more significant. Blifil hates Tom and is always scheming to undermine Allworthy's affection for him; so when he expresses his hopes of Tom's reformation, we understand that what he is actually doing is trying to maximise the damage that will be done by Tom's next transgression. We see clearly through Blifil's deceit, not because of anything we are told by the narrator, who as usual responds to the 'worthy young man' with bland credulity, but because of the hyperbolic character of the words that are presented as having been uttered by Blifil himself. It is easy to imagine that here too Fielding could italicise the expressions that identify the speaker's native dialect, which this time is the language not of Somerset but of hypocrisy: the *unparallelled* goodness of Allworthy *must certainly* effect a reformation in one not *absolutely* abandoned; if Jones *ever* offends again, Blifil will not be able to say a *syllable* in his favour. In the comic excesses of the rhetoric we can hear the tones of the author, sardonically pointing up the gap between the moralistic discourse and the malevolent intentions it serves. This is what Blifil is supposed to have said, but the words in inverted commas cannot be attributed to him in any absolute sense. They are also, or perhaps first of all, the instruments of an authorial discourse about false virtue.

This overdetermination of Blifil's words is not only the effect of a didactic intention on Fielding's part, but also a function of the fact that Blifil is, quite simply, the villain of the story: that is, he is bad where Tom is good, he prospers to the extent that Tom is unfortunate, he wants to marry the heroine, Sophia, who loathes him and is in love with Tom, and so on. Thus his speech is not the unmediated expression of an individual mind, even a wicked one; it is formed by its structural function of being the verbally articulated contrary of everything that tends to make the society of the novel just and happy. In other words, the dialogue, being part of the text rather than something outside it, consequently serves the text's requirements. Although it presents itself as speech, it is a literary production, shaped by literary genres and relationships. One more example, taken from the hero's words rather than the villain's, will indicate how this works.

Tom is in love with Sophia, but has a brief affair with the gamekeeper's daughter Molly. Some time after the affair has ended, there is a moment when Tom, a little drunk, is walking in a pleasant grove and thinking about Sophia:

> Oh! my fond heart is so wrapt in that tender bosom, that the brightest beauties would for me have no charms, nor would a hermit be colder in their embraces. Sophia, Sophia alone shall be mine. What raptures are in that name! I will engrave it on every tree.

(239)

He has his knife ready to do this when he happens to meet Molly:

> the girl coming near him, cry'd out with a smile, 'You don't intend to kill me, squire, I hope!' 'Why should you think I would kill you?' answered Jones. 'Nay,' replied she, 'after your cruel usage of me when I saw you last, killing me would, perhaps, be too great kindness for me to expect.'
>
> Here ensued a parly, which, as I do not think myself obliged to relate, I shall omit.

The dialogue here is entirely generic, and the genre is comedy. The exaggerated declaration of fidelity to Sophia has no point unless it is the prelude, as of course it is, to a quick roll in the bushes with Molly. The name of the rhetorical move is bathos: the sudden drop from the stylistically, morally, and socially high into the correspondingly low. The language spoken by both Tom and Molly is in the service of this comic effect. Tom's speech when he is alone is theatrical, both because it takes the form of a soliloquy and because its attitudes are at once extreme and conventional – that is, the writing is not character-ising Tom as an individual, but generalising him as a lover. The exchange between him and Molly is still closer to stage comedy, with the clichéd equation of rejection and death resolving into a sort of half-innuendo around the drawn penknife. They are speaking a literary dialect, and one might wonder how the uneducated Molly comes to be so fluent in it; but the objection is irrelevant because her lines, like Tom's, are dictated not by the consistencies of an imagined person, but by the requirements of the scene.

Once again, then, we see that, whatever the punctuation tells us, novelistic dialogue does not originate with its speakers, but is an instrument of the narrative. Its otherness is not really some-thing that novelists encounter, but something that they produce. The next questions, then, are about this production: how is the speech in novels made, out of what materials and under what conditions? These questions are on the home territory of one thinker in particular: the Soviet literary critic and philosopher Mikhail Bakhtin (1895–1975). To understand what he does with them, we will have to digress from the novel for a moment, returning to it in the section after next.

DIALOGIC LANGUAGE

This book is not an account of Bakhtin. He was the subject of several good introductions during the period of his Anglo-American ascendancy, which was the 1980s and 1990s; they properly cover several different topics, not only dialogue, and not only literary criticism either (Todorov 1984, Dentith 1995, Vice 1997). Nevertheless, 'dialogue' was a decisively important and productive term in much of his work, and it is his influence, more than anyone else's, that has made it part of the conceptual language of literary and linguistic studies across the world. The adjectives 'dialogic' and 'dialogical' still carry the trace of his thought, even when they enter, as they sometimes do, the deodorised environment of management consultancy; and the more exotic derivatives, such as the abstract noun 'dialogism' and the verb 'dialogise', owe their existence in modern English to his translators. His sense of the significance of dialogue, in the novel and elsewhere, is going to dominate the rest of this chapter, and to a lesser extent the rest of the book. To understand how he helps us with our enquiry, then, we do need an outline of who he was and what he did.

The setting of his whole working life was Soviet Russia. He was 22 at the time of the Revolution, and the fall of the Soviet Union was still in the future when he died at the age of 80. From 1918 to 1928, he was deeply involved in what is now known as 'the Bakhtin Circle', a group of young philosophers, linguists, and other scholars in the humanities, who met regularly to share findings, read papers, and discuss ideas (Brandist 2002). In the late 1920s organisations of this kind became impossible as Stalin tightened the state's grip on civil society. In 1929 Bakhtin published his first book, a study of the novels of Dostoevsky, but in the same year he was arrested and sentenced to five years' internal exile in Kazakhstan for suspected links with a religious discussion group. He lived in relative obscurity throughout the Stalin years, writing for the desk drawer until the 'thaw' of the

1960s. By then, all the other members of the circle were dead, and Bakhtin was unearthed as a sort of miraculous survivor from the early, experimental phase of Soviet intellectual life. Three major works came out of the drawer: a revised version of the Dostoevsky book in 1963, an extraordinary study of the French prose writer François Rabelais, written in the 1940s and published in 1965, and a collection of long essays centring on the history of the novel form, written between 1935 and 1941 and published in 1975. These books were translated into English as *Problems of Dostoevsky's Poetics* (1984), *Rabelais and his World* (1968) and *The Dialogic Imagination* (1981).

In this strange trajectory there is a motif that we can recognise from the dialogues of Plato or Castiglione: the elegiac image of past conversation. For over 30 years, Bakhtin developed on paper, often in exile and solitude, ideas that had previously been the currency of a circle of interlocutors. Unofficial but organised groups of this kind were a distinctive Russian tradition: in an authoritarian society with an undeveloped public sphere, they had significant cultural and ideological functions (Brandist 2002: 6–12). Georgii Gachev, one of the younger scholars who rediscovered Bakhtin in the 1960s, evocatively attributes his intellectual style to the particular kind of sociability that characterised his early milieu. 'They sat around the table all night and smoked and talked, smoked and talked' (Emerson 1997: 5) – that lost nocturnal space of tea and cigarettes and discussion is part of the context of what Bakhtin wrote about dialogue in the subsequent years of dictatorship and war. The group is called the Bakhtin Circle not because Bakhtin dominated it when it was in being, but because after it broke up, his circumstances and his determination made him its solitary voice.

This poignant and ironic relationship can be traced in a continuing uncertainty about the authorship of several books that appeared under the names of two other members of the circle, P.N. Medvedev and V.N. Volosinov. In particular, Volosinov's *Marxism and the Philosophy of Language*, published in 1929, pursues many of the same interests and problems as Bakhtin, and arrives at very similar conclusions. Different commentators have proposed different accounts of this connection: that Bakhtin wrote these texts and allowed Medvedev and Volosinov to take the credit; that Medvedev and Volosinov wrote them in collaboration with Bakhtin; that Medvedev and Volosinov wrote them independently but discussed them with Bakhtin while working on them; that Medvedev and Volosinov's books had a great influence on Bakhtin's later thinking. Deciding which of these theories is closest to the actual events is now very difficult and probably not worth the trouble. But the discussion is interesting from our point of view because of its similarity to the one about inverted commas. Once again, we have an apparently straightforward binary opposition: either the information on the title page of the book is correct and Volosinov is the author, or else it is not, and Bakhtin is the author. And once again, a little digging turns up a range of intermediate positions, redefining the simple alternatives as no more than the extremes of a continuum. The possibilities in the middle are effectively ways of saying that the book may be the product, not of either individual author, but precisely of a dialogue between the two. At this point the gossipy question of who wrote what meets up with Bakhtin's larger theme.

Broadly and initially it could be stated like this: dialogue is not, as this book has tended to suggest up until now, one particular use of language. Rather, dialogue is the universal condition of using language at all. It is impossible to say anything that does not pick up on something that was said earlier, and look out, hopefully or pre-emptively, for some kind of rejoinder. Everything that is said is part of an ongoing dialogue, and everything that is written too:

> Any utterance – the finished, written utterance not excepted – makes response to something and is calculated to be responded to in turn. It is but one link in a continuous chain of speech performances.
>
> (Volosinov 1973: 72)

In one reverberant word, verbal communication is inherently *dialogic*. Of course there are types of discourse, such as sermons, or private diaries, or monumental inscriptions, that appear on the contrary *mono*logic, in the sense that they have the air of a single person speaking while everyone else is silent or absent. But in fact even these address previous utterances and envisage subsequent responses, and so have a dialogic dimension. If they did not, they would have no impulse to communicate and no language to speak. As Volosinov puts it epigrammatically a few pages later, 'A word is a bridge thrown between myself and another' (86): unless the bridge is supported at both ends, it falls down and nobody gets anywhere. Dialogue is inescapable: the 'other' at the far end of the bridge always enters into the composition of what I loosely think of as *my* words.

In practice, my words are more and less than simply mine. For one thing, the bridge constitutes a sort of rhetorical imperative – what Bakhtin calls the 'orientation towards the listener and his answer' (*DI* 280). The 'listener' may be the literal addressee of a conversational remark or a personal letter, or the socially constructed virtual addressee of a published text, but in either case my intention of communicating with this figure shapes all my utterances; there is no discursive zero degree which would be *just* my 'own voice'. And anyway, where do I get 'my' words *from?* Not, as Bakhtin tartly observes, from the dictionary:

> rather [the word] exists in other people's mouths, in other people's contexts, serving other people's intentions: it is from there that one must take the word, and make it one's own. ... Language is not a neutral medium that passes freely and easily into the private property of the speaker's intentions; it is populated – overpopulated – with the intentions of others. Expropriating it, forcing it to submit to one's own intentions and accents, is a difficult and complicated process.
>
> (*DI* 294)

Putting the matter like that brings to consciousness an unspoken assumption that we each of us take our words from some central lexical storehouse where they are held in pristine condition, innocent of every context and intention, waiting for the next speaker to come along and make use of them. This vision is indeed widely entertained; it was explicitly endorsed, for example, by the Kingman Committee, which was appointed in 1988 to produce a model of the English language that could inform the curriculum in British schools. The report speaks of the need for a standard language:

> This must be the language which we have in common, which we call Standard English. All of us can have only partial access to Standard English: the language itself exists like a great social bank on which we all draw and to which we all contribute.
>
> (Kingman 1988: 14)

This sublime co-operative expresses, precisely, the dream of language as 'a neutral medium that passes freely and easily into the private property of the speaker's intentions'. Drawing on Standard English is apparently as simple as getting cash out of the wall: the bank has laundered the word so that it bears no traces of its previous transactions, and is now a universally convertible asset which you can spend on whatever you want.

Bakhtin reminds us of something at once obvious and oddly difficult to see: that this tranquil repository does not exist, that we must get the elements of our speech from other speakers, that these speakers will always be somebody in particular, and therefore that what we get from them will never be 'standard' English, but always a specific version of it shaped by their intentions and agendas. In short, that, in another Bakhtinian epigram, 'The word in language is half someone else's' (*DI* 293). He needed a term for this condition, and invented a new Russian word, which has been translated into a corresponding English neologism: *heteroglossia*. It is sometimes glossed 'diversity of speech types', which is accurate, but sounds too static. The point about 'heteroglossia' is not merely that different people speak in different ways, it is also that these different people speak *to each other*, and consequently that the diversity is always on the move, colliding, mutating, blocking and unblocking, generating little eddies of semantic agitation. 'Heteroglossia' could be more usefully defined, then, as *the way the word in language is always half someone else's*.

I think that this perception is one of the most exciting things about Bakhtin. It is not so much a theory or a set of propositions about language as a *way of imagining it*. Look for example at a selection of his metaphors for linguistic effects and events:

Discourse that has become an object is, as it were, itself unaware of the fact, like the person who goes about his business unaware that he is being watched.

(*PDP* 189)

When a member of a speaking collective comes upon a word, it ... enters his context from another context, permeated with the interpretations of others. His own thought finds the word already inhabited.

(*PDP* 202)

From this other discourse embedded in him, circles fan out, as it were, across the smooth surface of his speech, furrowing it.

(*PDP* 208)

From the very first sentence [of Dostoevsky's *Notes from Underground*] the hero's speech has already begun to cringe and break under the influence of the anticipated words of another. ...

(*PDP* 227)

The word, directed towards its object, enters a dialogically agitated and tension-filled environment of alien words, value judgments and accents, weaves in and out of complex interrelationships, merges with some, recoils from others, intersects with yet a third group.

(*DI* 276)

As these various analogies recur and accumulate in Bakhtin's writing, they build up an impression of discourse as an environment at once fluid, sociable, and risky. Bakhtin often uses the phrase 'the life of language', and language does appear in his account as something that has a life. Words possess consciousness, accommodate inhabitants, attract, repel, and intimidate one another; they are not given, but appropriated, alienated, permeated, fought over. Writing a novel or a poem, then, does not mean shaping an inert raw material like wood or clay; it means intervening in something that is already noisily going on. It is in this diffused sense that everything one does with words is dialogic. There are no innocent starting-points: the word has always been already used. The interrelating voices never converge on a conclusion: there is always more to say.

This sense of the omnipresence of dialogue in language is enlivening, but it throws up a difficulty that has troubled several interpreters. As David Lodge succinctly put it, 'If language is innately dialogic, how can there be monologic discourse?' (Lodge 1990: 90) If it is true that language use cannot help being dialogic, then monologic uses of language are impossible: there is no such thing as an authentically single voice. But then 'monologic' becomes an empty word, and that threatens to drain the force and precision out of 'dialogic' by depriving it of everything it could define itself *against*: if there is no discourse that is *not* dialogue, then 'dialogue' just means 'discourse'. This is not only a problem in abstract logic: it names a contradiction that recurs in Bakhtin's own uses of the term. In many passages, as we have seen, language as such is dialogic. But in the essays that make up *The Dialogic Imagination*, the novel is dialogic, and drama and lyric poetry appear by contrast as 'direct genres' or 'straightforward genres' (*DI* 43–50). And in *Problems of Dostoevsky's Poetics*, Dostoevsky is hailed as a pioneer of dialogic novel form, as opposed to monologic novelists such as Balzac or, especially, Tolstoy (*PDP* 34, 69–72). There are arguments to be had about these judgments of particular genres and writers; but what is striking right away is the contradictory *pattern*. The word 'dialogic' seems unsure of itself: in any given context, it denotes *both* a universal characteristic *and* one side of a binary opposition with 'monologic'. How can we overcome this instability, or at any rate live with it?

One route out of the difficulty is to point out that 'impossible' is not the same as 'inconceivable'. Although it is true enough that there is no such thing as monologic discourse, it is perfectly possible for a particular discourse to aspire to monologism, as it were: to resist the dialogic, to suppress the knowledge of its own antecedents and alternatives, to handle words as if their meaning were unitary and immutable, to prohibit every rejoinder and declare itself to be the final word. To the extent that a text behaves in this way, we could, without too much distortion, describe it as monologic; and that would allow us to describe as dialogic a text which, on the contrary, goes along with the inherently dialogic character of its medium, celebrating and inviting counter-words rather than struggling to silence them. A non-literary example might help with this important point.

In March 2009, a detachment of British soldiers was welcomed home from Iraq with a parade that was disrupted by demonstrators opposed to Britain's involvement in the war there. The *Daily Express* gave the demonstration a good deal of hostile coverage, and a couple of Islamist websites weighed in on the side of the demonstrators. A day or two later, the *Express* reported this response on its front page, under the headline: 'VILE FANATICS SAY OUR BOYS ARE COWARDS':

> Islamic hate preachers yesterday ridiculed British soldiers who were abused at a homecoming parade, branding them 'cowards' who have an 'uncanny knack for death by friendly fire'.
>
> Fanatical preacher Anjem Choudary and banned cleric Omar Bakri Mohammed praised Muslims who shamefully protested at the welcome home march in Luton for the 2nd Battalion Royal Anglian Regiment.
>
> In a sickening rant, Choudary cruelly mocked the soldiers' comrade who was killed by friendly fire in Afghanistan.
>
> He likened the soldiers to Nazis and branded Tuesday's homecoming a 'vile parade of brutal murderers'.
>
> (*Daily Express*, 12 March 2009)

This news story is wholly about the speech of others. Nothing has occurred since the parade, and the websites have advanced no new information either true or false. The only point of the splash is the *way* certain people have expressed themselves. This obviously requires two different discourses to be present on the one page: that of the website, which is being reported on, and that of the newspaper, which is doing the reporting. So far, it seems like a run-of-the-mill instance of 'dialogue' in Bakhtin's sense: the word responding to the other's word, and inviting a response in its turn. It is true that the two speaking groups, the preachers and the reporters, appear to loathe and despise one another. But it is important not to sentimentalise Bakhtin: he argued that dialogue is universal, not that it is necessarily either friendly or reasonable.

Nevertheless, the *Express* article is not dialogic in intention. This can be seen in the extreme difference in the presentation of the two discourses that make up the page. The newspaper's own utterance is as it were invisible: it admits to no positive character of its own, but asks to be taken as an unproblematic medium for impressions of the world. Thus, for instance, we are reminded that the protestors acted 'shamefully' in the same way as we are told that this happened 'in Luton'. Both qualifiers ask to be accepted as neutral vehicles of information; in both cases we are to see straight through the word to the truth of what happened. The preachers' prose, on the contrary, is not a medium at all, but entirely an opaque thing. It conveys no information, and it is represented largely in terms not of what it *says*, but of what it *does*: it ridicules, praises, rants, mocks, and brands. For example, take the report that Choudary 'likened the soldiers to Nazis'. Putting it like that gives no hint of what idea Choudary was seeking to communicate by this simile – his word does not appear as an instrument of thought, even wrong thought, only as a type of behaviour. In short, the newspaper's word *does nothing but represent*, and the preachers' word *does nothing but be represented*. Thus the dialogue which is latent in the story is systematically suppressed by the way it is told. In intention, the page is rigidly monologic.

The intention is especially conspicuous because, as it happens, it is not quite successfully executed. The most noticeable sign of stress, undermining the monologic regime, lies in the fact that *both* discourses make use of the word 'vile'. The *Express* calls the Islamic preachers vile fanatics, and the preachers call the home-coming ceremony a vile parade. 'Vile' is hardly a word in everyday use, nor is it simply a general-purpose insult; it expresses contempt as well as hostility, so it is appropriately applied to something trivially nasty, such as a parade or a website, rather than to the actual killing and dying in Iraq. It is also an archaic, vaguely Shakespearean word, which renders it a bit pretentious; you use it when you're striking a big public attitude. It does have a much more casual and colloquial use as a piece of Sloane-Rangerish slang, but the *gravitas* of both users keeps that register well out of earshot. In all these respects, Choudary and the *Express* are using the word in exactly the same way. The two voices do what both are concerned to deny: they *share* meaning.

This connection inadvertently undoes the monologic closure of the newspaper's rhetoric by rendering it reversible. Under its influence, for example, the headline conjures up a possible reader for whom 'our boys' are not the soldiers but the demonstrators who disrupted the parade. In other words, the two discourses on the page, which the writing is trying to fix in their respective subject and object positions, start to move in relation to one another, to admit that each knows the other is there, to get into a conversation. That is what is meant by 'dialogue'. In this case it is not meant to happen: the paper's front page is intended to be monologic. But it is difficult for it to escape dialogism entirely because, as Bakhtin says, that is what language is like.

It is appropriate that this example is a politically fraught one. Writing in the 1930s, Bakhtin had no need to spell out the political implications of the concept of monologism, and strong reasons for leaving them implicit. Monologic discourse, we saw a moment ago, is that which suppresses the knowledge of its own antecedents and alternatives, handles words as if their meaning were unitary and immutable, prohibits every rejoinder and declares itself to be the final word. In Stalinist Russia this was not a theoretically posited discourse with no actual existence; on the contrary, it was the everyday language of the state. To be sure, the dialogic principle is ultimately irresistible, but within the monologic framework, that fact is felt first of all in the vigilance and ferocity of the resistance to it. Analogously if much more trivially, the same logic is on view in the example from the *Express*. The article would *like*, as it were, to own its terms unconditionally, so that warm, positive words like 'British', 'home', and 'comrade', and judgmental, negative words like 'abused', 'coward', and 'brutal' would all alike express the values of an untroubled national solidarity. But the language community is more divided than that: as Bakhtin says, the words are found in alien mouths, and have to be extricated, appropriated, forced to serve the new speaker's purposes. This aggressive effort is then registered in the 'abuse' directed at the discursive enemy, who is 'fanatical', 'sickening', and 'cruel'.

So the *Express* hates the preachers, and in an irony that is becoming familiar, it expresses its hatred by calling them 'hate preachers'. The more the writing tries to widen the gap between its own words and the words of others, the more the words jump across it. And, of course, *vice versa*: the more the words jump across the gap, the more the writing tries to widen it. It follows that the attempt to purify one's language, to shake off all the heteroglot accents that cling to it, is in the end a violent one. The fact that monologic discourse is an unsustainable idea does not make it a negligible practice: on the contrary, it often exerts a dominance that is all the more oppressive because it is hostile to the nature of language.

DIALOGUE INTO NOVEL

The environment of the word is always dialogic, then, but some kinds of writing are more resistant to their environment than others. According to Bakhtin, the literary genre that resists the least, the one that finds itself most at home in heteroglossia, is the novel. What is the basis of this special sympathy between a literary form and the nature of language? What makes the novel *the* dialogic genre?

One way of pursuing this question is to ask about the novel's origins. It is, after all, a generic latecomer. Whereas forms such as tragedy and lyric stretch back to the beginnings of European poetry, the novel is a relatively recent invention: although there are some classical texts which can be retrospectively assigned to it, it was, as a genre, virtually unknown to the ancient and to the medieval world. So where did it come from? What are its literary ancestors and equivalents? What were the conditions of its emergence? Bakhtin calls this area of enquiry 'the pre-history of novelistic discourse' (*DI* 41–83). By putting it like that he clearly makes it a theoretical matter as much as an empirical one: the answer is determined not only by the novelistic traces literary archaeologists may unearth, but also by what they come in the process to mean by 'novelistic'. By looking for novel-like features in texts that are obviously not novels, we work out what we think novels are like.

One influential genealogy traces the novel's descent from epic. It works like this: during the famous discussion of imitation in Book 3 of Plato's *Republic*, Socrates argues that all poetry and story-telling may be said to be in one of three forms (Plato 1993: 394c). There are only three because the poet must necessarily speak either in his own voice or in somebody else's. If he speaks in his own voice he is a lyric or dithyrambic poet; if he speaks in the voices of others he is a dramatist; and if he does sometimes one and sometimes the other, he is an epic poet, like Homer in the *Iliad*. Epic, then, is the in-between form, in which the poet keeps switching between his own voice and those of the characters in his story. As we saw in some detail when looking at *Tom Jones*, this alternation is exactly what later distinguishes and animates the novel. Fielding himself, who had local reasons for disliking the term 'novel', described what he was writing as 'a comic epic poem in prose' (Fielding 1999: 49). Many subsequent critics, including Bakhtin himself, have developed this hint into an analogy between the great ancient and the great modern narrative form.

For Bakhtin, however, what the comparison reveals above all is that Homeric epic, seen from the standpoint of the novel, appears as definingly monologic. Sealed off from the give and take of current speech by its specialised verse forms and semi-mythical settings, it magnificently rebuffs the dialogic principle. The language in which the heroes express themselves is indistinguishable from the language in which they are described: they are already their legends. Their time is an 'absolute past', that is, not a past like yesterday that has a continuity with today, but the remote world of the first, the best of all, the archetype, 'walled off from all subsequent times by an impenetrable barrier' (*DI*, 17). A reverent 'epic distance' surrounds the characters, insulating them from any kind of verbal or ideological heterogeneity. One word for this self-complete verbal universe might be 'perfect'; another might be 'deaf'. In short, if this is the classical equivalent of the novel, it is an equivalent that specifically excludes what for Bakhtin is the most vital 'novelistic' element of all: dialogism.

He therefore looks for it elsewhere in the literature of antiquity, and one place he finds it, as we might expect, is in Socratic dialogue, the genre I considered at some length in the previous chapter of this book. Dialogue is of course not equivalent to the novel either: apart from anything else it is not a narrative form. But it contrasts with epic in interesting ways. Epic is in verse, dialogue in prose. Epic is set in a heroic past, the memory of which is the common property of the whole culture; the setting of the Socratic dialogue is contemporary, or a recent past preserved in the memory of an individual narrator. Epic poems are organised round the activities and values of princes; dialogues can accommodate the voices of tradesmen and schoolboys. The purpose of the epic is to relate great deeds, whereas the dialogue is open to random and trivial events: going out to dinner, meeting a friend in the street, discussing the latest music competition. It is easy to see how, in all these oppositions, dialogue anticipates the discursive world of the novel. The decisive distinction, though, and the one that generates the others, is that epic centrally represents actions, and its principal characters are what they are because of what they do, whereas dialogue represents speech, and its principal characters are what they are because of what they say: 'a speaking and conversing man is the central image of the genre' (*DI* 24). The same is true, less obviously but more profoundly, of the novel, whose primary purpose, according to Bakhtin, is 'to represent speaking persons and their ideological worlds' (*DI* 365).

This last proposition is not self-evident, and another example might help to clarify what is meant. Bakhtin describes *Don Quixote,* by Miguel de Cervantes, as 'the classic and purest model of the novel as genre' (*DI* 324), and many readers and writers have regarded it as the original novel. It was published in two parts in 1605 and 1615, and the first of many English translations appeared in 1616. That is, it was written when the Renaissance dialogue was still a living and vigorous genre, and this enables us to trace the connection Bakhtin suggests. Don Quixote is a country gentleman who reads too many romances about knights-errant, decides to become a knight-errant himself, and rides around the sixteenth-century Spanish countryside looking for distressed damsels to rescue from castles and wicked ogres to engage in single combat. He thus imagines himself to be the hero of a narrative of action, full of adventures in which the superiority of deeds to words is incontestably displayed. In fact, of course, his environment is devoid of the damsels, castles, and ogres his scenario requires. For much of the book, then, Don Quixote is engaged in an immense rhetorical struggle to redescribe the world so that it fits what he has read. The main vehicle for this project is his relationship with his almost equally famous squire, Sancho Panza. Sancho is a naive materialist who does not naturally see the world from the chivalric point of view, so as they ride along together, Quixote tries to teach it to him, and Sancho offers various kinds of resistance to his instruction. Thus the heart of the story is not heroic action after all, but a dialogue.

This is not simply to say that Don Quixote spends more of his time conversing than fighting giants, although he certainly does. It is also that he appears in the novel as the exponent of the *idea* of chivalry. In the stories he reads, chivalry is not an idea because it is the given condition of everything that happens; it is the air the characters breathe, and there is no room for differing opinions about it. But by dragging it into a discursive environment where it is not at home, Quixote turns this natural atmosphere into a theory about the world, a polemic against modern society, a code of conduct, a lifestyle choice: in short, he makes it into something that can be discussed. He therefore becomes what Bakhtin calls a 'hero-ideologue' (*DI* 38, 333–35), that is, a novelistic figure whose salience in the text, like that of a speaker in a dialogue, has to do above all with the ideas of which he is the voice and representative. Moreover, what the text does with these ideas is equally reminiscent of dialogue form: it 'tests' them. Dialogue in Plato appears as a mechanism for just this operation: Socrates asks people questions until he has provoked them into articulating their previously unspoken assumptions, and then questions them further in order to determine whether what they turn out to have been assuming is true. In much the same way, Bakhtin maintains, the plots of novels expose their hero-ideologues to interlocutors and circumstances that test the strength of both the hero and the ideology (*PDP* 109–12).

Don Quixote provides numerous examples to support this conception. The hero converses not only with Sancho, but with people who meet him on the road and are intrigued or provoked by his eccentric behaviour. One such inquirer, Don Diego, invites him home, where his son asks what the strange traveller is like:

> Said Don Diego, 'I know not what answer to make you; all I can say is, I never saw a madman act more franticly, and have heard him talk so very sensibly, as gave the lie to all his actions: but, I would have you enter into conversation with him, and sound the depth of his understanding.'
>
> (Cervantes 1998: 567)

'Sounding' someone's depths by entering into conversation with him is one of the most significant procedures which the novel derives from Socratic dialogue. The ensuing conversation is an illuminating sample of the method. Don Diego's son Lorenzo is an aspiring poet; Don Quixote courteously praises the dignity of this vocation, but claims that the profession of knight-errantry stands higher still, since the perfect knight must make himself expert in jurisprudence, divinity, medicine, and astronomy, besides the practical skills his adventurous life requires. He also needs to be morally exemplary:

> he must preserve his fealty to God and his mistress: he must be chaste in thought, decent in speech, liberal in action, valiant in exploits, patient in toil, charitable with the needy; and finally, an asserter of truth, even though the defence of it should cost him his life.
>
> (568–69)

Here Cervantes affords Don Quixote the ideological resources of Renaissance rhetoric: constructing knight-errantry as a combination of humanist learning, aristocratic honour and Christian virtue, he formulates, with easy eloquence, something quite close to the ideal that really did inform the ruling-class culture of the age. His speech is conventional, but it is precisely his command of the conventions that identifies him as a competent member of the speech-community, and contradicts the proposition (frequently advanced by the narrator as well as other characters) that Don Quixote is mad. The introduction of dialogue complicates the story by equipping the character to dispute the prevailing account of what he is like.

Lorenzo agrees that a discipline that led to all these virtues and accomplishments would indeed be the finest of all, but doubts whether knights-errant like this ever did or could exist. This qualification is his 'sounding'; he wants to see if Don Quixote replies with assertions so clearly at odds with reality that he can after all be written off as a lunatic. Quixote replies, however, that in his experience most people think the same as Lorenzo and cannot be persuaded otherwise, so he declines to try, but resolves to pray that Heaven will extricate him from his mistake; for his part, he believes that the wisdom of reviving the tradition of knight-errantry would be clear to all if the world were not sunk in sloth, gluttony, and extravagance.

> Here Don Lorenzo said within himself, 'Now hath our guest given us the slip; but, nevertheless, he is a whimsical madman, and I should be an idle fool, if I thought otherwise.'

Then dinner is announced, so with this reflection the conversation ends. Don Lorenzo decides that Don Quixote is mad, but his turns of phrase – 'nevertheless', 'if I thought otherwise' – indicate how closely the opposite conclusion is pressing upon him. In other words, this silent utterance of Don Lorenzo, commenting on his dialogue with Don Quixote, is itself caught up in a further dialogue he is having with himself. It is as if one inner speaker has said 'Perhaps this severe critic of sloth and extravagance is not as mad as people think', and the other inner speaker replies 'Don't be such a fool!'

Thus we can see how dialogue provides the structuring principle for the episode, and for many comparable encounters between Don Quixote and the people around him. But it does not follow that novel and dialogue constitute a single genre, or even that the novel is simply incorporating the dialogue genre entire, as it often incorporates other written forms, such as songs or letters. What marks the difference is precisely the uncertainty in which Don Lorenzo is left: as the narrative voice emphasises, he *can't make Don Quixote out*. The puzzle represented by the guest's reasonable speeches and demented actions is explored but not solved; the situation that prompts the dialogue cannot as it turns out be reduced to the dialogue's explicit content. There is more; and what produces this excess, according to Bakhtin, is that in the novel, the dialogue is not fundamentally between two comparable points of view, as it would be in a rhetorically organised disputation. It is between two *languages* (DI 399–400).

Don Quixote is an exceptionally clear example of this because it names the language of the hero with such unqualified specificity: it is the language of the chivalric romances which have turned his brain. It can be called a language, not merely a set of literary conventions, because *once the hero has decided to speak it,* it constitutes a complete alternative terminological repertoire for constructing the world. This begins with his name. In the Spanish society described by the narrator, he is not even Don Quixote, since he is a country squire who is not entitled to call himself Don anything, and his name is thought to be Quixada or something like that, but he is so obscure that nobody is certain. But in the chivalric world he chooses to inhabit, he is the renowned Don Quixote de la Mancha, Knight of the Rueful Countenance and Knight of the Lion; and by the same token, a local girl he once fancied is the beautiful princess Dulcinea del Toboso, the inn where he stays the night is a castle, the landlord is its Steward, the whores hanging around in front of it are damsels taking the air on the terrace, and so on. It is a question, not of two opinions which could be adjudicated according to a common system of measurement, but of two systems of measurement. Hence the vitality of *both* of them as the story progresses, despite the fact that one of them is absurd. The hero's insanity is the stroke of genius that splits the representational code irreparably in two, but also ensures that its incommensurable fragments get snarled up with one another whenever he encounters anything in the world around him – that is to say, the whole time. So the two languages can be neither merged nor separated. Permanently at odds, they bother each other with questions, interruptions, commentaries, jokes, critiques, negations, translations: in one word, their relationship is a dialogue.

It is this dialogue of languages that Bakhtin regards as fundamental to the novel form. Passages in which characters talk to each other appear in his account as 'manifest dialogues', or on one occasion 'mere conversations', surface traces of the dialogic structure that underlies and always exceeds them:

> Dialogue in the novel. ... can never be exhausted in pragmatically motivated dialogues of characters. Novelistic dialogue is pregnant with an endless multitude of dialogic confrontations, which do not and cannot resolve it, and which, as it were, only locally (as one out of many possible dialogues) illustrate this endless, deep-lying dialogue of languages.
>
> (*DI* 364–65)

Don Quixote and Sancho Panza talk about courage or cheese or the people they have just encountered, and that is 'dialogue in the novel' in an incidental sort of way: they could equally talk about something else, or ride along in silence, or the narrative could simply skip to the next adventure. What Bakhtin more seriously means by 'dialogue in the novel' is the undescribed, 'endless, deep-lying dialogue of languages' which constitutes the novel itself, and of which the 'manifest' dialogues are one expression. It is this dialogue-producing dialogue – this novelistic dialog*ism* – that we will examine next.

THE DIALOGUE OF LANGUAGES

If the novel is the natural literary venue for a 'dialogue of languages', one reason for this is its extraordinary inclusiveness. Most classical genres have formal conventions which effectively control the importation of other discourses: tragedy proscribes jokes, lyric makes everything fit its metrical scheme, satire demands a low style, and so on. The novel, by contrast, keeps open house: sermons, essays, poems, letters, diaries, shaggy dog stories and newspaper reports can all come as they are. Too disparate to impose its own discourse, the novel accepts alien ones, not troubling to assimilate them to their new environment, or to efface the traces left on them by their previous functions. So the genre's formal openness makes it a sort of compendium of language in use.

Historically, this miscellaneity is part of the novel's formation. In a few months in 1823–24, for example, major works appeared from the three founding writers of Scottish fiction: John Galt, James Hogg, and Walter Scott. Galt's *Ringan Gilhaize* (1823) is supposed to be the autobiography of a Covenanter, a Protestant fighter who lived through the civil wars from 1638 to 1689. The whole book imitates as closely as it can the language, the range of experience, and the point of view of its chosen historical type: its aim, you could say, is to be mistaken for a real seventeenth-century memoir. Hogg's *Confessions of a Justified Sinner* (1824) is another fictional Calvinist autobiography, but it is presented as a psychiatric document rather than a historical one: it seems that the writer was a madman, or a victim of diabolic possession, whose manuscript has been recovered from his grave and is now published with assorted proofs of its authenticity and an extended editorial introduction. Scott's *Redgauntlet* (1824) tells the first half of its story through an exchange of letters between its two young heroes, and later features a legendary tale told to one of them by a blind fiddler who is wholly distinct, in dialect and viewpoint, from either the letter-writers or the third-person narrator who takes over from them. In this moment in the novel's formation within one national culture, then, it can be seen to have no generic language of its own. Instead, it borrows the languages of autobiography, antiquarianism, periodical journalism, religious tract, familiar letter, and folk narrative. A 'diversity of speech types' is literally what it is made out of.

There is more to 'diversity', though, than a miscellaneous wardrobe of verbal costumes. In the sense Bakhtin intends, a language is not just a freely available way of talking or writing; it is organically attached to a particular profession, generation, religion, faction, class, or the like, encoding the group's distinctive values and securing its shared identity. So when a novel adopts a language, it is adopting a verbal and ideological *world*. This is clear enough from our trio of Scottish novels. As we saw in passing when looking at David Hume, eighteenth-century Edinburgh was an Enlightenment capital with an older culture of religious militancy. The two discourses persisted in tension well into the nineteenth century. The language of the political and intellectual establishment tended to be classical, eirenic, anglicised, oriented towards a commercial and imperial future; the language of faith Biblical, polemical, Scots, oriented towards a heroic national past. The religious language is reproduced in each of these novels – Galt imitates it with respectful accuracy; Hogg subjects it to grotesque and ambivalent parody; Scott, through the medium of his blind story-teller, renders it picturesque. Thus all three novels are exploiting the same historically charged opposition of discourses, engineering disjunctions of language which are in the same breath disjunctions of value. The 'dialogue of languages', then, is not an abstract generic feature; it is a form of the novel's participation in the divisions and interactions of its society. In Bakhtinian shorthand: novelistic dialogue has its roots in social heteroglossia.

As the Scottish example suggests, this social participation is not passive. The three writers all have the same verbal–ideological object in view: the language of native seventeenth-century religious radicalism. But they all do definite and different things with it: copying, parodying, picturing. Each strategy represents a different relationship with the historically given discourse. In other words, what is in question is not the simple presence of another's intonation, reflected or assimilated in the novel, but an encounter between *two* languages: the Calvinist rhetoric and the authorial narrative, the represented language and the language that represents it (*DI* 359). In this type of encounter, according to Bakhtin, the word is penetrated by authorial intentions while still serving those of the represented speaker. It therefore belongs to both languages at once: it is the scene of a conversation between them, that is, it is *dialogised*. For Bakhtin it is this internal dialogisation, rather than any amount of external conversation, that gives the novel its uniquely dialogic character. The dialogue that really matters takes place inside the words.

To see how this idea might work in detail, I shall once again take several examples from a single novel: this time, *Bleak House*, by Charles Dickens, first published in 1852–53. This is the book whose famous satiric target is 'Jarndyce and Jarndyce', the interminable lawsuit in the Court of Chancery. Unsurprisingly, then, one of its dominant 'verbal-ideological worlds' is the law. But that puts it too narrowly: Chancery in the novel is not a single issue but the symbol of a whole social formation. The Court itself was a fifteenth-century foundation whose independence was meant to enable it to transcend the errors of more strictly regulated jurisdictions; but over time it accumulated such a weight of procedure on its own account that by the mid nineteenth century it was doing little except collecting customary fees and reducing litigants to despair. For Dickens, then, its continuance is a spectacular instance of *privilege*, that is, the arbitrary exemption of a particular person or institution from normal standards of fairness and humanity. The basis of privilege is antiquity; throughout the novel, people and institutions are shown demanding special treatment, and enjoying special authority, merely because they have been around for a long time. The Court of Chancery thus appears as the centre of a web of indefensible privileges, an ancient social order seen from a vigorously reforming point of view.

The character who mainly represents this order is the conservative grandee Sir Leicester Dedlock. In plot terms he has no involvement with the case of Jarndyce and Jarndyce, but his ideological link with it is made early:

> Sir Leicester has no objection to an interminable Chancery suit. It is a slow, expensive, British, constitutional kind of thing. ... [H]e regards the Court of Chancery, even if it should involve an occasional delay of justice and a trifling amount of confusion, as a something, devised in conjunction with a variety of other somethings, by the perfection of human wisdom, for the eternal settlement (humanly speaking) of everything. And he is upon the whole of a fixed opinion, that to give the sanction of his countenance to any complaints respecting it, would be to encourage some person in the lower classes to rise up somewhere – like Wat Tyler.
>
> (Dickens 1948: 13)

Formally, this gives Sir Leicester's views in indirect discourse, telling us what he 'has no objection to', how he 'regards' the

Court, what his 'fixed opinion' is. And sometimes it gives them in what may be imagined as the words he would use. For example, the acknowledgment that Chancery may 'involve an occasional delay of justice and a trifling amount of confusion' is effectively a fragment of direct speech. The elevated viewpoint from which the Court's monstrous inefficiency looks like a minor imperfection is clearly Sir Leicester's. So is the oratorical symmetry between the paired phrases: his voice is often marked syntactically like this, elaborate subordinate clauses and ponderous connectives affiliating him to the official language of the establishment, as if he were a *Times* editorial walking about.

So this is what Volosinov calls 'texture-analysing' indirect speech: that is, it gives not only an account of what the character thought or said, but also an impression of his characteristic movements of mind and turns of phrase (Volosinov 1973: 130–32). But only a very unsuspicious reader would leave it at that. The same sentence also has the structure of a *joke*:

> [H]e regards the Court of Chancery, even if it should involve an occasional delay of justice and a trifling amount of confusion, as a something, devised in conjunction with a variety of other somethings, by the perfection of human wisdom, for the eternal settlement (humanly speaking) of everything.

It is bathos: the grandiose build up, through the regarding and the parenthetic clause, leads you to expect an idea, but then, instead, you get 'a something' conjoined with 'other somethings' for the settlement of 'everything'. In the sudden drop into total vagueness, and especially in the comic plural form of 'something', the reader detects, not Sir Leicester's consciousness, but a mocking authorial consciousness *of* him. In exactly the moment that the impressive rhythm of the sentence assigns it to the authorship of Sir Leicester, the choice of noun announces the intervention of a second author, aggressively unimpressed. It is what Bakhtin calls 'double-voiced discourse'. Two distinct speakers are heard in the same words, one signalled by the syntax, the other by the vocabulary.

The prize of this particular example, though, comes in the earlier and simpler sentence: 'It is a slow, expensive, British, constitutional kind of thing.' Chancery is denounced by reformers like Dickens exactly because it is slow and expensive; here the same words express Sir Leicester's approval of it. The novel shows how this valuation emerges from a mode of life. Everything about Sir Leicester is slow and expensive: he moves slowly because he is too privileged to need to hurry, his syntax is so magnificent that it takes him a long time to say anything, the pace of life on his country estate is leisurely, with ancestral trees maturing and servants remaining with the family for generations. 'Slow and expensive' in this context connotes aristocratic dignity: only vulgar people would admire something for being fast and cheap. Thus opposing sets of values, opposing political agendas, even opposing social classes, literally meet in the interior of two commonplace adjectives. The words, in short, are internally dialogised.

The *content* of the dialogue is the broad difference between the two social languages in play, but its *mechanism*, the device that brings them to talk to each other and not just sit monologically side by side, is reported speech. As Bakhtin emphasises, transmitting the speech of another is always also recontextualising it, reorganising it in a new frame (*DI* 340). In order to say what somebody else said, I must necessarily speak myself; and my new utterance has its own context and intention which cannot help being superimposed upon the different context and intention of the former speaker. This routinely happens not only in novels but also in ordinary life, including the life represented in novels. This fact is particularly salient in *Bleak House* since, of course, the practice of law often does involve paraphrasing things that other people have said.

At the far end of the social scale from Sir Leicester Dedlock is Jo the crossing-sweeper, who is so bereft of every kind of resource that he counts as the schematic opposite of privilege: he is the novel's unaccommodated man. At a crucial point in the plot, a man known to Jo dies, and the Coroner questions him to determine whether he can give evidence at the inquest:

> Name, Jo. Nothing else that he knows on. Don't know that everybody has two names. Never heerd of sich a think. Don't know that Jo is short for a longer name. Thinks it long enough for *him*. *He* don't find

no fault with it. Spell it? No. *He* can't spell it. No father, no mother, no friends. Never been to school. What's home? Knows a broom's a broom, and knows it's wicked to tell a lie. Don't recollect who told him about the broom, or about the lie, but knows both. Can't exactly say what'll be done to him arter he's dead if he tells a lie to the gentlemen here, but believes it'll be something wery bad to punish him. ...

(148)

The grammatical mode of this is, once again, indirect speech: it is to be understood as a third-person account of what Jo said. But this time, the 'original' that we are to infer from the report is itself a dialogue: the paragraph enables us to reconstruct not only Jo's utterances, but also the questions that prompted them. It is therefore almost a paradigm of dialogisation: by folding the interaction of two speakers into ostensibly monologic form, the writing drives the dialogue of languages inwards, concentrating in terse, conflict-filled phrases the heartbreaking mismatch between the two 'verbal-ideological worlds', the Coroner's and the boy's, the established discourse of the law and the terminological helplessness of the crossing-sweeper. The questions are designed to elicit the normal qualifications of a competent witness: name, address, signature, next of kin, comprehension of what it means to testify on oath. Jo's failure to produce any of these elementary markers of civic identity is a sort of unintended satire on the categories into which the Coroner is trying to fit him: according to the language of the court Jo has no demonstrable existence, and yet here he is. The court naturally responds to this anomaly by concluding that there is something wrong with Jo; the other side of the dialogue raises the alternative possibility that there is something wrong with the language.

But this brilliantly compressed meeting of languages is not the primary dialogic encounter here. The formal model for the passage is the newspaper reporting of court proceedings: at the time Dickens wrote *Bleak House*, several examinations of exactly this kind had just been printed in papers he worked for (Fielding and Brice 1968–69). His immediate language-object, then – the discourse that directly confronts the author as another's – is neither the witness's speech nor the coroner's, but a certain kind of transcript. Dickens was in fact a shorthand reporter for six years before becoming a novelist, and here it is as if the narrator rapidly assumes the role of a stenographer taking down the boy's answers: 'Name, Jo.' But then what this act of impersonation instantly generates is an internal dialogue. There are so to speak *two* shorthand reports on the same pad: an official one on behalf of the inquest, and an unofficial one on behalf of the novel. The writer of the first is only concerned with the work of the court; the writer of the second has the novel's unlimited interest in human lives, and so opens up words the first writer intends to be final. For example: 'Spell it? No. *He* can't spell it.' For the official report, the content of this is simply the information that Jo cannot spell his name. But the unofficial reporter intervenes to italicise 'he', and so to introduce a personal note: is *he* (of all people) likely to be able to spell? how would *he* acquire such an ability? is *he* ever going to be in a situation where it would be of any use to him? Thus the official language is teased, disconcerted, dialogised. The most decisive effect is when Jo, badgered with questions, asks one himself: 'What's home?' Presumably he has been asked where his home is, and doesn't understand the question. The official reporter enters 'N/A' and moves briskly on; but the unofficial reporter stops for a second to gaze into the abyss of a fellow human being to whom the word 'home' conveys nothing. Jo's utterance is thus noted and overlooked at the same time, and that momentary divergence alerts us to the fact that the narrative is double-voiced. The dialogue between Jo and the Coroner is underpinned by the more inward dialogue between different ways of recording it.

These examples of dialogism in the novel clarify one further point that can become confused. Bakhtin is sometimes taken to be demanding that a novel's characters be, as Wayne Booth puts it in an admiring preface, 'respected as full subjects' (*PDP* xxiii) rather than subordinated to the tendentious views of the author. On this interpretation of his categories, the 'monologic' novelist is the one who reads us lectures and tells us unambiguously which characters we are to admire and which to disapprove of; whereas the 'dialogic' novelist frees the characters to speak for themselves, and the readers to come to their own unconstrained conclusions about who is right. If this were indeed the significant distinction, then *Bleak House* would be a poor example of dialogism. Dickens usually makes it clear who his heroes and villains are, and the dialogic encounters I have examined in detail (aristocratic and democratic, judge and vagrant) are not in the least even-handed: on the contrary, the discourses of privilege are being subjected to passionate and unambiguous attack. What renders the writing dialogic is not authorial acceptance of the character's point of view, but authorial orchestration of the character's speech-world in such a way that however unacceptable it may be, it engages with the narrative, it makes its presence felt within it, it *answers back*. Don Quixote is mad, Sir Leicester Dedlock is a pompous fool, some of the Dostoevskian protagonists studied by Bakhtin are psychopaths. That does not stop them being carriers of a fully articulated language that enters the 'deep-lying dialogue' of the novel.

As it happens, this can be demonstrated negatively by turning to the end of Sir Leicester's story. At the climax of the plot, his wife is exposed to public disgrace and runs away in an effort to spare him the shame. He is devastated, but recovers sufficiently to make a speech to his relatives, which is given in direct discourse. He realises, he says at the end of it, that his lady may have enemies because of her high position:

> Let it be known to them, as I make it known to you, that being of sound mind, memory and understanding, I revoke no disposition I have made in her favour. I abridge nothing I have ever bestowed upon her. I am on unaltered terms with her, and I recall – having the full power to do it if I were so disposed, as you see – no act I have done for her advantage and happiness.

> (794)

Read as an image of speech, this is unmistakably the Dedlock language we already know: it has the same declarative egocentricity and pedantically placed parenthetic clauses; and it evokes legal language too, through its echo of the standard opening of the text of a will. But here this discourse, which Dickens has been mocking for hundreds of pages, is revived in order to articulate a heroic act of forgiveness and love. The sequence, then, is a moment of ambivalence after all, when the accent of privilege comes rather to suggest honour, or unworldliness, and so the reformer's denunciation is deflected.

But although this complication in the authorial ideology is interesting, it is not dialogic. There is no gap between what the character wants to say and what the author wants to say about him: the same words serve both intentions without strain. Brought to a level of common humanity by his misfortunes, Sir Leicester ceases to offer any discursive resistance to the flow of authorial understanding: the narrator explains that although his 'formal array of words' might be ridiculous at any other time, now they are 'simply honourable, manly, and true.' With the disappearance of that discursive tension, the writing gravitates towards monologism: author and characters are enfolded in a single, truly named world. The condition of dialogism turns out to have been, not an Olympian authorial acceptance that every language has its own validity, but just the opposite: a loquacious partisanship, roaming about the complicated verbal field of the novel and starting arguments. Crucially, the 'dialogue of languages' is not merely an openness but a conversation; not something the author believes, but something the writing *does*.

THE IDEOLOGY OF DIALOGUE

It is evident by now that 'dialogism' is not a neutral descriptive concept but an expression of value: Bakhtin is as it were writing not only about but *for* dialogue. When he says the novel is a dialogic form, he is praising it; when he contrasts the dialogical Dostoevsky with the monological Tolstoy, he is arguing that Dostoevsky is a better novelist. For example, he speaks about him in these terms:

> Dostoevsky's works contain no final, finalizing discourse that defines anything once and for ever. ... Discourse of the hero and discourse about the hero are determined by an open dialogic attitude toward oneself and toward the other. Authorial discourse cannot encompass

the hero and his word on all sides, cannot lock in and finalize him from without. It can only address itself to him. All definitions and all points of view are swallowed up by dialogue, drawn into its becoming ... 'Secondhand' discourse providing a final summary of personality does not enter into his design. Whatever is firm, dead, finished, unable to respond, whatever has already spoken its final word, does not exist in Dostoevsky's world.

(*PDP* 251)

The implicit opposition is vividly polemical: the monologic is final, locked, second-hand, dead, unresponsive, silent, whereas the dialogic is characterised by openness, relationship, and becoming. Dialogism is thus the carrier of a set of general values: interplay rather than certainty, incompleteness rather than perfection, change rather than stasis, heterogeneity rather than unity. Clearly these are not just literary preferences but ethical and political ones: in other words, they potentially make the 'novelistic' into an *ideological* theme, as if there is something, or a set of things, that people who like novels *believe in*. This ideology of the novel recurs in twentieth-century criticism, and at least in the English-speaking world it is a liberal one. In the late 1940s, for example, Lionel Trilling effectively looked to the novel as the cultural anti-dote to totalitarianism (Trilling 1951), and F.R. Leavis embraced it as the form of felt and responsive life in society as opposed to its schematisation by doctrinaire or scientistic social models (Leavis 1948). An eloquent contemporary champion of the form, James Wood, centrally praises it as the medium in which we escape from our dogmatic selfhood and understand the complexity of being someone else (Wood 2008). Philip Pulman places himself in the same tradition when he argues that theocracies hate reading because of its cultivation of ambivalence, independent-mindedness, and dialogue (Pulman 2004).

So we can identify a valorisation both of dialogism and of the novel, which Bakhtin did not originate, though it may well be one reason why his work was so readily assimilated into the Anglo-American literary academy. A widespread, not very highly theorised feeling associates the writing and reading of novels with secular liberal politics. This feeling was dramatically actualised in the late 1980s when one particular novel – Salman Rushdie's *The Satanic Verses* – came into direct conflict with an apparently antithetic set of beliefs (Ruthven 1990). By looking back on some aspects of this complicated and still reverberant controversy, we can see some of what is at stake.

The Satanic Verses, published in September 1988, tells of two Indian characters who, fantastically precipitated into London, undergo surreal transformations. One of them, Gibreel Farishta, is a Bollywood movie star of Muslim extraction who loses his faith; internally contaminated by a hysterical feast of pork, he experiences twisted dreams about the life of Muhammad, who appears under his demonising medieval European name, Mahound. The narration of these dreams, which takes up two of the novel's nine chapters, struck some readers as shockingly blasphemous, and this reaction was communicated to many others who had not read the novel but heard about its more lurid statements and images. The book was banned in several countries with large Muslim populations; in England a series of demonstrations demanded that the UK government should do the same. Then, in February 1989, the spiritual leader of the Iranian revolution, Ayatollah Khomeini, raised the stakes enormously by calling on Muslims to kill Salman Rushdie for his crime against Islam. Rushdie went into hiding with Special Branch protection, and stayed undercover for nine years. Appalled readers and writers across the world made public statements in support of him.

One of these, by the Mexican novelist Carlos Fuentes, began by citing Bakhtin to the effect that the novel is 'the privileged arena where languages in conflict can meet':

> This is no gratuitous exercise. It reveals a number of things. The first is that, in dialogue, no one is absolutely right: neither speaker holds an absolute truth or, indeed, has an absolute hold over history. Myself and the other, as well as the history that both of us are making, still are not. Both are unfinished and so can only continue to be. By its very nature, the novel indicates that we are becoming. There is no final solution. There is no last word. ...
>
> But this is precisely what the Ayatollahs of this world cannot suffer. For the Ayatollahs, reality is dogmatically defined once and for all in a

sacred text. But a sacred text is, by definition, a completed and exclusive text. You can add nothing to it. It does not converse with anyone. It is its own loudspeaker.

(Fuentes 1989)

This is Bakhtin's opposition in schematic form. The dialogic unfinalisability of the novel finds its opposite in the idea of a 'once and for all' sacred text; conversely, then, novelistic discourse comes into new focus as the opposite of the sacred. The novel is the definingly *un*sacred text, proudly impure and provisional, the special form of secular modern (not to say postmodern) consciousness. At the heart of the 'Rushdie affair', on this view, is a collision between two kinds of text: the theocentric and the decentred, the authoritarian Quran and the libertarian fiction.

Fuentes' account of the Quran is obviously hostile, but it is not simply false. The Quran in Muslim tradition is indeed a sacred text in a full and serious sense. It is the word of God, communicated by Him to the Prophet Muhammad. It is therefore absolutely unique: all other texts come into existence by entirely different means. It is also absolutely finished: when the Prophet died in 632, it became permanently impossible to add or subtract a single character. And as a matter of fact, given its life in countless scribal copies over a thousand years between its first revelation and its first printing, it has shown astonishing textual stability: it seems to be literally immune to change. Even translation, though necessary for some practical purposes, is traditionally regarded as a dubious sophistication of the text: the Quran is given in Arabic, and only the Arabic Quran is the true one. There have been interesting differences within Islam on the question of whether or not the Quran was created: the dominant view seems to be that it was not – that is, that it did not come into being at a moment in time like the things of the world, but exists eternally, like God Himself, and was merely *revealed* at a moment in time. If that is so, then the Quran is a specific exception to Bakhtin's principle that the first and last words of all are never uttered. The divine word is both. If there can despite everything be a truly monologic discourse, this is it (Cook 2000, Zakaria 1991).

And yet a connoisseur of the dialogic might look at this differently. The Prophet's immediate source was not God Himself, but an angel who put the verses into his mind; Muhammad recited them, and his companions wrote them down. Within the text, this indirectness takes the form of a variation in the voicing: some verses address Muhammad, so that the constructive speaker is God or the angel, while others begin 'Say' or 'Tell the people' and go on to specify what Muhammad should say to others, so that the constructive speaker is human, and God appears in the third person. Moreover, because of this personal mode of transmission, the text is full of inexplicit allusions to biographical details or cultural references that Muhammad the addressee can be assumed to understand. These need explaining; so a densely layered tradition of commentaries has evolved to annotate and interpret the original. It is not certain how far such commentaries should adopt historicist methods. On the one hand, since the text is divine, human history is irrelevant to it. On the other hand, God was addressing the people of a particular epoch, and therefore adopted their language and adapted His message to their assumptions, so to that extent, philological or ethnographic research can have a bearing on our understanding after all. The line between God and man seems to run through the middle of the words.

In all these ways, the sacred word seems less like a self-complete monologue which 'is its own loudspeaker', and more like an intricate network of dialogic relations between angel and prophet, script and recitation, eternal and historical, text and commentary. Precisely because the Quran's exact meaning has mattered so much to so many people for so long, it is impossible for it to maintain a position in which 'it does not converse with anyone'. On the contrary, it is embroiled in a conversation that never ends. Monologic as it appears, the text has a richly dialogic underside, which makes the insistence on its immutability, its self-guaranteed completeness, look like a gesture of repression.

It is this denied dialogic potential that Rushdie mischievously sets out to expose. His point of entry is provided by the story of the Satanic verses themselves. According to an apocryphal tradition, one day when Muhammad was receiving the sacred word, he was in a despondent mood because of his failure to win over the polytheistic inhabitants of Mecca. He had told them that there is only one God, but they were attached to their multiple deities: how could he overcome their hostility and convert them? Satan took advantage of his doubtful state of mind to smuggle into the angel's dictation a couple of extra verses in praise of a trio of pagan goddesses, which Muhammad duly recited in the city. The polytheists were delighted by this unexpected courtesy, but Muhammad soon realised that he had been deceived, and was full of remorse. Elsewhere in the true Quran, God implicitly comforts him: Satan is always trying to contaminate the truth, and not even the holiest prophets are immune. For the faithful in general, the point of the story is the Prophet's error and its forgiveness: no-one is to be worshipped except God, for even Muhammad was only human (Cook 2000: 128–29).

For the novelist, on the other hand, the point of the story is the multiple relationships that infiltrate and dialogise the ostensibly sacred word. The Prophet's recitation is a response to God, to Satan, to the angel, to the public, to his own inner speech, and to his followers and amanuenses, who often disagree with one another. On top of all that, he is also in a political situation: the Grandee, the head of the city's governing council, is trying to do a deal with him, and the Grandee's glamorous wife is an uncompromising devotee of one of the goddesses. Thus, instead of the sovereign text that it is for Islam, the Quran appears as the tension-filled site of a conversation between a dozen different speakers and interests, its singleness farcically swallowed up by dialogue.

Even the divine voice is dialogised. In the film star's dream he becomes his namesake Gibreel (or Gabriel), so we get the canonical encounter, the very origin of the Quran, from the slightly panic-stricken point of view of the angel: '*Not my voice* I'd never know such words I'm no classy speaker never was never will be but this isn't my voice it's a Voice.' (Rushdie 1988: 112) Where do the words come from? It is the very question that we saw leading Bakhtin to the concept of heteroglossia. Officially, the origin of these particular words is absolutely pure and single; but novels, as we have seen, live on the basis that words come from multiple and conflicted places. A bit of God, a bit of Satan, a bit of the movies. After he has delivered the verses about the goddesses, Mahound returns in anguish to Gibreel, wrestles with him until his doubts are resolved, and eventually goes away in a state of certainty: now he *knows* that the problematic verses were from Satan, and all the rest are from God. But Gibreel, left on his mountaintop, watches him go and thinks *'it was me both times, baba. ... '* (123) *Novelising* the story undoes the categorical distinction between divine and satanic verses, opening up the play of ambiguities prophetic discourse tensely suppresses.

Thus novel form, with its characteristic structures and procedures and jokes, appears within the book itself as the enemy of Quranic authority. The external storm that followed its publication looks, in retrospect, specifically predictable from its internal climate. One of a number of rather spooky premonitions concerns Salman the Persian, a companion of the Prophet who, in another distorted memory of a traditional story, starts making experimental alterations to the Quran as he writes it down. When Mahound fails to notice the emendations, Salman loses his faith in the text's divinity and runs away, but when Mahound conquers the city he is captured and condemned to death:

> Mahound shakes his head. 'Your blasphemy, Salman, can't be forgiven. Did you think I wouldn't work it out? To set your words against the Words of God.'
>
> (374)

Setting their words against the words of God is what both Salmans have effectively been doing: the novelist's demure self-reference compounds the offence by drawing even his own condemnation into the babble of fictionalised and parodied voices. To that extent, the outraged response was not based on a misreading. The dialogic is indeed being advanced, consciously, in opposition to Islamic orthodoxy.

However, this militancy is not without its contradictions. Making dialogue itself into a polemical function has the effect of inhibiting its freedom to work as dialogue. It makes dialogism into something one champions: we are, as it were, on the side of dialogue. This necessarily generates the *other* side: dialogue's adversary, the anti-dialogic. However, as soon we have constructed this adversary it becomes our only significant dialogic inter- locutor. For example, if we say, like Philip Pulman, that the anti- dialogic principle is called 'theocracy', then everything around the assertion of the dialogic tells us that theocracy is the other; so if there is to be dialogue, how can it be with anything except theocracy? But then it is difficult to establish a dialogic relation- ship with what has just been defined as the negation of dialogue. So in the very moment of its triumph over theocracy, dialogue ceases to dialogise and starts turning into its contrary. Implicit behind the dream chapters of *The Satanic Verses* is a discourse of Muslim piety: a voice saying that God is the Lord of all Being, the All-merciful, the All-compassionate, that Muhammad is His Prophet, that the Quran is His uncreated word, and so on. This voice must be there, because the chapters make no sense without it: it is what they are written *against*. But it cannot be heard; the novel has no mechanism for sounding it; it is present only as unsaid, or gainsaid.

Take the moment I quoted earlier, when Gibreel begins to reveal the Quran to Mahound:

> It happens: revelation. Like this: Mahound, still in his notsleep, becomes rigid, veins bulge in his neck, he clutches at his centre. No, no, nothing like an epileptic fit, it can't be explained away that easily; what epileptic fit ever caused day to turn to night, caused clouds to mass overhead, caused the air to thicken into soup while an angel hung, scared silly, in the sky above the sufferer, held up like a kite on a golden thread? The dragging again the dragging and now the miracle starts in his my our guts, he is straining with all his might at some- thing, forcing something, and Gibreel begins to feel that strength that force, here it is *at my own jaw* working it, opening shutting: and the power, starting within Mahound, reaching up to *my vocal cords* and the voice comes.
>
> (112)

As we have seen, this is all *about* the dialogical reality of the supposedly monologic sacred text. Everything is doubled. Mahound is both Muhammad and his medieval travesty; Gibreel is both the archangel and the dreaming film star; the self-consciously unstable pronouns advertise the confusion of boundaries between the two already hybrid characters; the impending utterance is grotesquely interactive, with Mahound forcing Gibreel to reveal to him, as from Heaven, messages that come from inside Mahound himself. But the *writing* has no dialogic relationship with another consciousness, another's discourse. Mahound is present only physiologically, as what bulges, clutches, strains: what he is presumably experiencing is a life-defining miracle, his meeting with the messenger of God, but there is no notation for his consciousness, his 'world'. Gibreel is almost equally absent: the loose dream convention frees his inner speech from every potential identity. He has a half-Americanised Bombay patois which characterises him after a fashion, but this appears intermittently and for comic effect; he is sometimes given a high 'angelic' point of view in a cinematic sense, but this comes and goes in the same whimsical way. And so on: the fact that Gibreel can sound like anything effectively leaves him voiceless. Consequently, there is nothing to resist the dominant discourse, which remains that of the entertainer-narrator, with his impressionistic punctuation, his verbal facetiousness and his conjuror's patter. Thematically preoccupied with doubling, this is, nevertheless, firmly single-voiced discourse. It talks about dialogue, but it does not engage in it.

What is deployed against the sacred word, then, is not so much dialogic discourse as the idea of it. The style is a sort of rhetoric of heteroglossia, a deliberate riot of discordant tones that advertises the novel's commitment to multiplicity. But beneath the polychromatic surface there is a single, sustained authorial intention. This subtle gap between what the narrative sounds like and what it does is a reminder that the dialogic, in Bakhtin's sense, is constituted not simply by doing different voices, but by their semantically charged action upon one another, interpreting, animating, translating, answering back:

> [Monologic] authors cast a mantle of objectivity over every point of view they do not share, turning it, to one degree or another, into a thing. In contrast to this, Dostoevsky's authorial activity is evident in

his extension of every contending point of view to its maximal force and depth. ... And this activity, the intensifying of someone else's thought, is possible only on the basis of a dialogic relationship to that other consciousness, that other point of view.

(*PDP* 68–69)

Once again, it is not about sympathy. Dostoevsky's 'intensifying of someone else's thought' includes thoughts to which, authorially, he is explicitly and contemptuously opposed: the dialogue may be an angrily hostile one. Conversely, 'a dialogic relationship to ... that other point of view' is absent from Rushdie's novel despite his unquestionable and heroic commitment to the values of cultural diversity and freedom of expression: the monologue may be a friendly and open-minded one. It may even be in the name of dialogue that the author casts his objectifying mantle over the opposing (anti-dialogic) point of view. The extent to which the novel really operates as a dialogic form is determined not by the author's opinions, but by the text's capacity to get its heteroglot voices to interact. A book in praise of dialogue can still disappoint Alice by proving to be a book without conversations.

3

DIALOGUE IN DRAMA

BAKHTIN ON DRAMA

In Bakhtin's view, drama is an inherently monologic mode of writing. Of course that sounds paradoxical. Surely drama *consists of* dialogue, the scripted interaction of different voices? And if it is a question of generating a Bakhtinian 'dialogue of languages', an interanimating encounter of several verbal-ideological worlds, what plainer or more forceful method could there be than to put each one into the mouth, literally, of a different speaker, and arrange for them to meet and question and answer one another? Bakhtin is familiar with this line of thought, but unconvinced by it:

> [T]he dramatic dialogue in drama and the dramatized dialogue in the narrative forms are always encased in a firm and stable monologic framework. In drama, of course, this monologic framework does not find direct verbal expression, but precisely in drama is it especially monolithic. The rejoinders in a dramatic dialogue do not rip apart the represented world, do not make it multi-leveled; on the contrary, if they are to be authentically dramatic, these rejoinders necessitate the utmost monolithic unity of that world. In drama the world must be

made from a single piece. ... The whole concept of a dramatic action,
as that which resolves all dialogic oppositions, is purely monologic.

(*PDP* 17)

The world of the novel, as we saw, does *not* need to be 'made from
a single piece'. It can be made from several pieces, that is, from
the discourses of the several speakers and narrators who intersect
with one another at various semantic levels of the text. In drama,
on the other hand, there is, besides and behind the discourses
of the more or less differentiated speakers, a single, shared world
which they all inhabit. This world is not itself a discourse; rather,
for the purposes of the drama, it is simply the way things are.
The characters may of course express differing attitudes towards
it: in fact, one influential doctrine states that they *must* express
differing attitudes towards it, because drama presupposes conflict.
But these differences cannot become truly dialogic, for two reasons.
First, the play's languages, insofar as they are diverse or antithetic, are each contained by the separate bodies of the actors, and
dialogisation is therefore impossible. There are no double-voiced
words in drama, because each word is categorically assigned to
one voice or another. And anyway, second, dramatic characters
are constituted not by what they say, but by what they do. Drama
is essentially the imitation of an action, as Aristotle says and
critics endlessly repeat; as a result, what is said in a play always
defers, in the end, to what happens in it (Aristotle 1965: 39–40).
The public are not readers who are told about the action; they are
spectators who watch it. In the shadow of this supremacy of the
event, dialogue is a secondary affair: whatever anyone says, it is
not going to 'rip apart the represented world'. Consequently,
dramatic structure classically converges on a moment of truth,
when the misunderstandings are cleared up, the evasions are
exhausted, and the whole cast, assembled on the stage, see the
same reality and speak the same language. It is, Bakhtin argues, a
profoundly monologic destination.

Although Bakhtin made this point several times in different
contexts, he still leaves a suspicion that it is not quite what he
thinks about plays, or at least not quite all that he thinks about
them. In 'Discourse in the Novel' he says, again, that 'dramatic

dialogue is determined by a collision between individuals who exist within the limits of a single world and a single unitary language' (*DI* 405), but then a footnote explains that he is speaking 'of pure classical drama as expressing the ideal extreme of the genre', and the next sentence in the text adds that 'to a certain extent comedy is an exception' as well. Ideally, then, drama is monologic, but actual drama does not always conform to the ideal. Some of the other possibilities make a fleeting appearance in a dimension of Bakhtin's work that I mentioned earlier: the 'prehistory' of novelistic discourse. Among the forerunners of the novel's heteroglot fluency, he argues, are low, popular parodies of high discourses:

> It is precisely here, on a small scale – in the minor low genres, on the itinerant stage, in public squares on market day, in street songs and jokes – that devices were first worked out for constructing images of a language, devices for coupling discourse with the image of a particular kind of speaker.
>
> (*DI* 400)

Or again:

> on the lower levels, on the stages of local fairs and at buffoon spectacles, the heteroglossia of the clown sounded forth, ridiculing all 'languages' and dialects; ... where all languages were masks and where no 'language' could claim to be an authentic, incontestable face.
>
> (*DI* 273)

At moments like this, it seems that dialogism has something atavistically theatrical about it: its primitive models are the fairground stage, the clown who apes his betters, the performer in a mask. The drama that is always monologic, then, is haunted by another drama, wilder, 'lower', and latently dialogic, which is kept at arm's length by uneasy formulations such as 'pure drama' or 'drama in the strict sense'.

The uneasiness does not prove that, as some critics have announced, Bakhtin was simply wrong about drama (Stam 1989: 16, seconded by Pearce 1994: 82). Rather, he has two conflicting accounts of it. But both accounts are illuminating in their different ways: after all, stage dialogue is a complicated phenomenon. So in this chapter I shall take each in turn. First the grounds and implications of a conception of drama as monologic; then the objections and exceptions. First 'pure' drama, then the impurities.

PURE DRAMA

What would *pure* drama be? Go back for a moment to the three possibilities proposed by Plato: the poet speaks consistently in his own voice, or he consistently adopts the voices of others, or he does sometimes one and sometimes the other. If drama is the second of these modes, then it is 'pure' drama when there is no admixture of authorial intonation at all, when the poet *in propria persona* is completely silent. This is the most straightforward way of grasping what Bakhtin means by describing drama as monologic. As we saw, what particularly makes novels dialogic is the manifold interpenetration of authorial and characteral voices in the field of indirect speech. In pure drama, on the contrary, there is no authorial voice and all the speech is direct. So each character is heard uninflected, uninterrupted, *single* voiced. Paradoxically, then, drama is monologic precisely because its verbal texture consists of nothing but dialogue.

This conception of drama is luminously articulated by Peter Szondi at the opening of his *Theory of the Modern Drama* (Szondi 1987: 7–11). In a formulation very like Bakhtin's, Szondi calls it 'absolute drama'; and although that makes it sound like a sort of logical essence, he immediately adds that, in fact, it is a historical practice of a fairly specific kind. Most theatres have *not* put all their eggs in the one basket of interpersonal communication. Classical Athens is normally thought of as the birthplace of European drama, but there, individual interacting speakers shared the time and space with the stronger and more spectacular presence of the Chorus. The human actors of medieval religious drama were framed by ritual and didactic pronouncements addressed directly to the public. Comic performers, from folk-drama clowns to TV-oriented stand-up comedians, have always moved fluidly between speaking in role and speaking in person. In short, pure drama, where no word is spoken that is not the dialogue of fictional persons in a fictional situation, is not a universal dramatic norm but a special case. According to Szondi's synoptic account, it was formed in the world-view of Renaissance humanism, dominated the poetics of European drama through into the nineteenth century, and then, with the advent of Ibsen, Strindberg, and Chekhov, entered the crisis of validity we call 'modern drama'.

The operating requirement of pure drama is that every message from the playwright to the audience has to pass through the medium of the words spoken to one another by the dramatis personae. If the story includes an object that does not in itself have this interpersonal character – God, a wet afternoon, a fall in interest rates – the playwright cannot invoke it directly, but must 'dramatise' it, that is, arrange for it to feature allusively in the interaction of the characters on the stage. If a writer fails to meet this requirement, and breaks the frame of dialogue with over-extended narrative, or over-explicit polemic, or under-motivated exposition, the effect is described as 'undramatic', which means that the disappearance of the authorial word into those of the characters is incomplete; the dialogue is wearing thin; the writer is showing through and making us uneasy. In derivatives like 'dramatise' or 'undramatic', the idea of 'drama' continues to exert a prescriptive force, denoting not stage writing in general, but the dramaturgic regime that is characterised by 'the absolute dominance of dialogue' (Szondi 1987: 8). Other voices, other ways of communicating, are absent not because they are inherently unstageable, but because this particular dramatic convention rules them out. 'Undramatic' utterances are not impossible; on the contrary, it is because they are possible that they need to be prohibited.

We could say, then, that drama renders itself absolute by proscribing narrative. Drama is a story with no storyteller. Of course it is permissible, even usual, for dramatic dialogue to include narration: people recount what has happened offstage, or before the play began. But in that case the story they tell is precisely not the story the play tells: if the tragedy of Dido and Aeneas includes Aeneas' account of the fall of Troy, the event in the play is not 'the Greeks burn the city' but 'Aeneas tells

Dido a story'. In other words, pure drama has no past tense; it lives in an absolute temporal and spatial present; it never tells, it shows. This mutually exclusive opposition of drama and narrative has contradictory implications for stage dialogue. On the one hand, it means that the words spoken on the stage are cut off from the play's own representational processes. They are uttered and understood wholly within the world of the play, and cannot create or alter it. The characters of absolute drama do not narrate themselves to us; they behave, and we observe them, and the things we hear them say are part of their behaviour in just the same way as the things we see them do. But then on the other hand, we have already noted that the playwright forgoes every means of narration *except* the words spoken by the characters on the stage. So far from being cut off from the business of creating the world of the play, the dialogue is its sole medium; it carries the whole weight of the story as novelistic dialogue is not usually expected to do. Taking everything into account, then, dialogue seems to be absolutely central to drama and at the same time entirely incidental to it.

The mechanism that reconciles this contradiction is familiar to literary criticism as 'dramatic irony'. Traditionally, this is the effect of a line of dialogue that is understood by the audience in a sense of which the speaker is unaware. The text-book example is the moment early in Shakespeare's *Macbeth* when the treacherous Thane of Cawdor is executed. The king reflects sadly that he was wrong about the Thane: 'He was a gentleman on whom I built / An absolute trust,' he says, and then is interrupted by the entrance of Macbeth, whom he at once greets affectionately, and who will shortly murder him (1.4.13–14). This is an elegant example because nobody in the play perceives the meaning that is so obvious to the audience: not the king and his courtiers because they do not suspect Macbeth of treachery, and not Macbeth himself because he arrives on stage too late to hear the line. The author has smuggled a message to us through the speech of his characters *without their knowledge*.

That is a famous example because it is exceptional and pointed, but the same structure, the same ironic conjunction of significance and unawareness, is the *normal* condition of purely dramatic dialogue. Take a much more run-of-the-mill passage, the opening of Arthur Miller's early play *All My Sons* (1947):

JIM: Where's your tobacco?
KELLER: I think I left it on the table. *Jim goes slowly to table in the arbour, finds a pouch, and sits there on the bench, filling his pipe.* Gonna rain tonight.
JIM: Paper says so?
KELLER: Yeah, right here.
JIM: Then it can't rain.
Frank Lubey enters,
FRANK: Hya.
KELLER: Hello Frank. What's doin'?
FRANK: Nothin'. Walking off my breakfast. *Looks up at the sky.* That beautiful? Not a cloud.
KELLER: *looking up* Yeah, nice.
FRANK: Every Sunday ought to be like this.
KELLER: *indicating the sections beside him* Want the paper?
FRANK: What's the difference, it's all bad news. What's today's calamity?
KELLER: I don't know, I don't read the news part any more.

(Miller 1961: 90)

I have borrowed this example from Keir Elam's book about the semiotics of drama, where it is quoted to illustrate the dramatic use of 'deixis' (Elam 1980: 141). This is the linguistic term for expressions that point at objects in the immediate context of utterance, and in some way depend on the objects for the completion of their meaning. Thus: if I say 'Does anyone mind if I shut it?', I am trusting to the non-verbal context to make it clear that 'it' is a nearby window, and that the reference of 'anyone' is restricted to the people I am addressing. I am using 'anyone' and 'it' *deictically*. On the stage, deixis often works in a peculiar inverted way, because the circumstances that are being pointed at are not real, and the deictic constructions are designed to produce the illusion that they are. The incomplete meanings finesse the audience into supplying from its imagination the objective world that would complete them. Elam is right: this extract is full of examples of this manoeuvre: 'right here'; 'tonight'; 'that beautiful?';

'like this'. The curtain has just gone up, and Miller is building a solid, circumstantial play-world out of unobtrusive deictics.

But the condition of this exposition is the same as that of the irony in *Macbeth*: an extreme disjunction between what the characters are saying to each other and what, in the same words, the playwright is saying to the audience. What is idle chat for them is plot stuff for us. There is a fine example of this in Frank's first line: 'Nothin'. Walking off my breakfast. *Looks up at the sky*. That beautiful? Not a cloud.' To summarise the narrative information here would take more words than there are in the line. It is morning; it is sunny; it is an exterior scene; Frank is a neighbour; these are men with a good deal of leisure. But of course it is not Frank who is communicating these facts; he is talking to people who are already familiar with all of them. He is the oblivious instrument of Miller's communication with us.

This goes further than exposition. *All My Sons* is a tragedy; in its final seconds Keller will shoot himself. So the cloudless sky and the forecast of rain connect the opening, a little portentously, to the larger generic design. Moreover, the didactic purpose of the play as a whole, signalled in its title, is an attack on the privatisation of morality: what Miller is concerned to say to the audience, as it were editorially, is that we have ethical responsibilities not only to our families but to our wider society, which we ignore at our peril. So the business with the newspaper in this scene, full of bad news that no-one will read, makes a light, early statement of the main message – a statement which, once again, emanates not from any of the characters on the stage, but from the author.

Thus an apparently artless and inconsequential piece of dialogue is shot through with authorial intentions; the characters, who in their own terms are just lazing about, are working hard for the play. In a way, this analysis is spelling out the obvious: this is how we expect plays to work, or at any rate the plays of a particular time and convention, the plays of absolute drama. One interesting aspect of it from our point of view, though, is the empowerment of the author. The dramatis personae are, definingly, unaware; their words have no power to confer meaning on their experiences, but are observable symptoms of their more or less false or partial consciousness. The authoritative interpretation of events, on the other hand, comes in coded messages from the dramatist, which the dramatis personae cannot read even though they are the messengers. By Miller's time, this drastic subordination of the character could appear as a compositional rule: a contemporary manual tells aspiring dramatists, 'The best playwrights are those who use words obliquely, who let the character speak without being aware of what he is saying.' (Weales 1964: 61)

Thus the disappearance of authorial discourse does not mean that the author loses his authority. On the contrary: the fact that his meanings have no direct verbal embodiment helps to render them unquestionable. As James Joyce famously puts it, the dramatic writer is like the God of creation: he expresses himself not in his own words but in the entire structure of his world, which includes everybody else's words (Joyce 2000: 181). There is therefore no conceivable ground on which the voices of author and hero could meet dialogically, since the hero is not a subject of knowledge, but purely an object of the author's knowledge. In this kind of theatre at least, when Bakhtin maintains that 'dramatic dialogue in drama [is] always encased in a firm and stable monologic framework', it is difficult to protest that we do not see what he means.

DIALOGUE AS ILLUSION

When critics resist the contention that drama is monologic, it is sometimes because they hear it as crushingly judgmental, as if a literary text that fails to be dialogic is therefore a failure in every way. I do not think that was Bakhtin's opinion, and even if it was, we are not obliged to share it. Purely dramatic dialogue may be always 'encased in a firm and stable monologic framework', but it is not all the same. Sometimes it works, sometimes not; so what are its conditions of success?

The terms of evaluation form an interesting starting point in themselves. People always seem to know what constitutes 'good dialogue'. In 1912 the drama critic William Archer judged that 'the average quality of modern dialogue' had greatly improved over the previous 30 years (Archer 1926: 293). In 2008 a *New*

York Times review could say: 'no one writes better dialogue than Richard Price – not Elmore Leonard, not David Mamet, not even David Chase' (Kakutani 2008). Here the measure for a novelist is provided by another novelist, a dramatist, and a screenwriter. The quality of dialogue, it seems, is a value that floats free of the texts in which the dialogue appears; like roller-blading or mixing cocktails, it is just something that some people are good at. This makes dialogue-writing into what Archer liked to call a craft: not so much an element in an artistic vision of the world as a skill you can practise and master.

One reason for this is that in absolute drama, dialogue has the character of a *trick*. Sentences composed by the author are made to sound as if they are the spontaneous utterances of the people on the stage. The audience know that this is not so, but they enjoy the sensation of being deceived. So the writer of dialogue is a kind of illusionist, like a conjuror or a ventriloquist. The trick may be hard to do, but it is easy to say whether or not it has been done, and easy to say, therefore, whether the performer is good at it. If he is, the puppets appear to move and speak of their own volition; if not, not. That would be to say: writing good dialogue means *producing the illusion that the characters are the origin of what they say*.

For Archer himself, this is a fairly straightforward matter. The reason earlier playwrights wrote bad dialogue was that they had not learned how to conceal its writtenness. Extended metaphors, ingenious puns and high-flown declarations made it painfully obvious that the actor was not taking part in a conversation, as we were asked to suppose, but reciting a literary composition. It was necessary for a generation of playwrights to learn how to simulate the vocabulary and rhythms of actual speech. This conception of the task is still influential. Especially in naturalistic television drama, where the filming techniques imitate documentary, and the objects that appear on the screen are as far as possible not merely realistic but real, speech tends to become one more such object. The characters' dialogue is, as Steve Gooch says, 'hanging on them like a coat', and so the verbal idiom, like the coat, has to be recognisably something the viewers can imagine wearing themselves (Gooch 2001:51). The talk in the play should sound like talk in life: that is the trick the writer of dialogue is asked to execute.

This correlation is not without theoretical support: there is for example a small academic genre that applies linguistic theories of spoken discourse to the study of plays. These theories are based on the assumption that ordinary conversation has implicit rules that can be extrapolated from the way people behave when they are talking to each other. By analysing transcripts of actual conversation, linguistic researchers have hypothesised principles that govern things like turn-taking, face-saving, and criteria of relevance. It is then possible to explore a play by treating the script as if it were a transcript, and enquiring whether its fictional conversationalists are observing or violating or manipulating these immanent rules.

This procedure may sound as if it entails a naive belief that the dramatis personae are real people, but it does not. Rather, the rationale is that although dramatic dialogue is obviously not the same thing as real conversation, it is designed to resemble it; and to the extent that it does so, the audience make sense of it by drawing on their own conversational expertise. Understanding a real-life interlocutor, after all, means inferring their intentions, their implications, their interiority, from more or less fragmentary conversational cues. Your identity, in Vimala Herman's precise phrase, is my 'inferential accomplishment' (Herman 1995: 200). It is by the *same* process that an audience attributes identity to the fictional speakers in a play. If dramatic dialogue did not resemble our own conversation (so the argument goes), it would resist our strategies for interpreting it and the play would be unintelligible.

All the same, the conception of dramatic dialogue as an *imitation* of conversation has serious limitations. Whenever it is examined empirically, for example by comparing a sequence from a contemporary play with a transcript of real tape-recorded talk, the two things turn out to be radically different (Elam 1980: 178–84). The difference is registered in surface linguistic features: even naturalistic written dialogue has an artificial verbal texture; it spells out more of its allusions than real conversationalists tend to do; it has more thematic coherence; its 'turn-taking' is more orderly; and so on. But these things are only corollaries of the decisive distinction, which is that real conversation is autonomous, whereas dramatic dialogue is shaped at every moment by the requirements of the play. That structural relationship is what a purely mimetic model of dramatic speech is doomed to suppress. By connecting the dramatised word to a supposed original in real life, it abstracts it from what is happening on the stage. This produces incoherence because, as we saw earlier, drama consists of present action; so it is precisely in its relation to action that dramatic dialogue lives or fails to live. If we are to stay with the notion that 'good dialogue' is a matter of producing the illusion that the characters are the origin of the lines they speak, we need a more relational model for this effect than the idea of copying speech patterns.

DIALOGUE AS ACTION

One such model, which has influenced both the practice of theatre and its academic theorisation, is founded on the concept of the speech act. This goes back to J.L. Austin's famous essay in the philosophy of language, *How To Do Things With Words*, first published in 1962. Austin pointed out that philosophers sometimes tacitly assume that language is descriptive, as if the only thing we ever do with words is to make true or false statements about the world. Against this assumption, he highlighted a category of utterances that are neither true nor false but 'performative'. For example, if I write in my will, 'I bequeath my watch to my brother', I am not describing anything, but doing something. The same applies if I say to a friend, 'I bet you a pound it rains tomorrow'. The utterance is not a statement about betting, it *is* betting; the thing the sentence means is performed in the act of speaking it. Rather than 'true' or 'false', performatives may be judged 'happy' or 'unhappy', depending on whether the action in question is successfully accomplished (Austin 1975: 12–14).

Austin's thesis has a peculiar shape, because it is partly an ambitious theory of language and partly a whimsical footnote. On the one hand, his class of performatives is small and slightly bizarre (naming a ship, getting married, challenging somebody to a duel). But on the other hand, the *idea* of an utterance which is also an action is so fertile that it threatens to account for the whole of communicative activity, demolishing altogether the common sense distinction between words and deeds. Once you reflect, after all, you see that the range of things we do with words goes well beyond Austin's initial examples. As he points out himself in later chapters, we promise, thank, apologise, censure, approve, welcome, congratulate, often though not automatically by using those very words. And even discourses that purport to be factual description, and therefore do inhabit the world of truth and falsehood, nevertheless also have their performative dimension: we argue, testify, conclude, concede, predict, and so on. In the end, it seems that a 'speech act' is not so much a particular communicative event as a particular way of looking at *any* communicative event, albeit a way whose defining paradigm is still found in the eccentric group of ceremonial functions with which Austin began. Coming to this conclusion, Austin formulates it by saying that if any utterance can be thought of as a 'locution' (that is, what is said), it is also in the same breath an 'illocution' (that is, what saying it does). The aspect of an utterance that works like a performative, then, is its 'illocutionary force' (98–108).

It is easy to see in principle how this notion might find itself at home in the theatre. So far from undermining drama by abstracting the word from the action, it connects the two things in the most radical way by conceiving of speech as a *form* of action. As an early 'speech-act' critic put it, 'the action [of the play] rides on a train of illocutions' (Ohmann 1973: 83). Moreover, it exactly fits the definition of pure drama. As we saw, pure drama is the opposite of narrative: it distinguishes itself from other kinds of literary representation by its absolute *presentness*. The actors on the stage are not to tell us about happenings in some other time and place, but to enact them for us here and now. This is the same choice as Austin's: a focus not on the referential function of words, their orientation towards something outside themselves, but on their immediate force, the event which is constituted by their being spoken. 'Speech act theory' invites us to consider the lines of the play, not primarily as a source of information about the fictional world or about anything else, but as something the characters are doing.

Perhaps the purest examples of what this can mean dramaturgically are provided by Pinter, whose best-known plays were first performed between 1957 and 1965, and so are closely contemporary with *How To Do Things With Words*, which was presented as a series of lectures in 1955 and in book form in 1962. Take the opening of *The Homecoming* (1965):

MAX: What have you done with the scissors?
    Pause.
    I said I'm looking for the scissors. What have you done with them?
    Pause.
    Did you hear me? I want to cut something out of the paper.
LENNY: I'm reading the paper.
MAX: Not that paper. I haven't even read that paper. I'm talking about last
    Sunday's paper. I was just having a look at it in the kitchen.
    Pause.
    Do you hear what I'm saying? I'm talking to you! Where's the scissors?
LENNY: [*looking up, quietly*] Why don't you shut up, you daft prat?

                                                       (Pinter 1965:7)

If *The Homecoming* acknowledged the same conventions as *All My Sons*, the objects referred to here would be significant in some way: the fact that the scissors are missing would be the trace of a crime, or the information Max has found in the newspaper would have a bearing on the plot. But that is not what is happening at all. What these characters are talking *about* is merely instrumental to the talking itself, the brutal interplay of speech acts. For example, what makes Lenny's first line funny? It is not easy to spell out, but it goes something like this. His initial silence makes us wonder why he fails to acknowledge Max's question. Is he asleep? or too preoccupied to hear? or is he not on speaking terms with him? Then his line brings all these possibilities crashing comically down by revealing that he has been listening with critical attention all along. Not only that, but it is also funny because of the way he goes unerringly for the side issue. Max's main point is that he wants to know where the scissors are; only when repeated demands get him nowhere does he resort to explaining what he wants the scissors for, as if that strengthened his case for demanding an answer. Lenny instantly homes in on this rather feeble expedient, attacking the subsidiary explanation in a way that nudges the primary question out of reach. His response has the character of a feint: Max expects resistance around the scissors and is wrongfooted by a counter-attack via the paper, as his flustered reaction shows.

The interchange is made up not of statements but of *moves*: requesting, demanding, explaining, ignoring, revealing, attacking. The word suggests a game, and the scene does have something of the content-free immediacy of sport. Lenny's startling aggressiveness is not so much an expression of emotion as a style of play. In other words, this is to an extreme extent a theatre of illocutions: one where our attention is almost entirely concentrated on the characters' present actions, but the foremost medium of those actions is language. Charged with this performative task, the word is referentially weak: what we hear about the back-story or the off-stage world is shadowy and unreliable, and the intermittent messages from the characters' inner lives are similarly dubious. Speech is not information: the act is all.

Dialogue like this does the trick: it produces the illusion that the characters are the origin of what they say. But it does so not because it approximates especially closely to 'real' speech. (The baroque-sadistic idiom of a figure like Lenny is hardly something you hear every day.) Rather, it is that each line is a move the speaker is making in the game against the others. It is 'good' dialogue because it is integrated in the action to an unprecedented degree: rather than constituting a literary intrusion in the world of the play, like the dialogue Archer recalled from the 1880s, it is so devoid of autonomous literary significance as to be *nothing but* the audible form of the characters' interaction.

The idea of illocution, then, establishes the dramatis personae as separate speakers on the basis of their conflicting intentions within the world of the play. Perhaps because of this power to connect subjectivity and action, it has made its most explicit theatrical impact not on dramatists but on actors. A rehearsal technique called 'actioning', associated with the theatre directors Max Stafford-Clark and Mike Alfreds, asks the actors to prepare their roles by labelling each line with a verb that names the action of the words (Stafford-Clark 1989: 66–68). Strictly speaking, it should always be a first person transitive verb, so that the focus stays on what the speaker is doing *to* the interlocutor. Thus, an actioning of the opening of *The Homecoming* might go (treating the pauses as Lenny's lines):

MAX: I accuse you.
LENNY: I ignore you.
MAX: I remind you.
LENNY: I ignore you.
MAX: I reason with you.
LENNY: I correct you.

Working this out together helps the actors identify the rhythms of their interaction, and clarify what each utterance is trying to effect. At its simplest, the theory is that actors will speak their lines more accurately and forcefully if they know what they are doing. At its most far-reaching, it leaves no scrap of text that is not animated by someone or other's distinctive intentionality; the entire script is resolved into interpersonal dynamics; it is the utopia of pure drama.

Harold Pinter and Max Stafford-Clark do not make the same kind of theatre, but their different practices both represent a specifically illocutionary version of staged speech. My impression is that it continues to be widely influential. Steve Gooch, for example, tells his students that speaking should be the last thing a character does: 'It should be almost as if the lines were forced out – from sheer necessity, that there is such an urgency in the situation ... that speech is the only solution' (Gooch 2001: 63). Val Taylor, also teaching playwriting, has a similar conception: 'Dramatic characters always speak for a reason: where they don't have one, they shouldn't speak' (Taylor 2002: 116). Both these maxims effectively situate the essence of a line of dialogue in the interpersonal predicament that can be thought of as causing it to be uttered. What matters about a speech is not what it says exactly, and certainly not how witty or thought-provoking or true it is in itself, but its intelligibility as an action performed by the character who speaks it. Making it seem that the characters are the origin of what they say is not merely a trick: it is the centrepiece of a dramaturgic orthodoxy.

In a sense, this is the triumph of a dialogic principle. What seals the connection between word and actor is not an individualised conception of appropriateness to character, or the psychologically imagined interiority a person's utterances are supposed to express: it is the interactive to-and-fro of power and feeling and desire *between* the dramatis personae. They are each of them what they are because of their verbal interaction with the others: the characters are to that extent dialogically constructed. Moreover, this interactivity produces a 'naturalness' that owes nothing to conversational naturalism. So long as the dialogue maintains its organic connection with the action, it can be conducted in any idiom at all – fanciful Hiberno-English, rhyming couplets, rhythmic grunts. Its function is not to imitate anything, but to be the medium in which characters affect one another and define themselves.

Yet for all its aptness and power, it is hard to resist a feeling that the image of a play as 'a train of illocutions' has something narrow about it, something tight-lipped. It is symptomatic, for example, that actioning has the effect of subordinating the *whole* of the text to a scenario of unspoken moves and countermoves. It is as if, *ex hypothesi*, characters *never* realise their meanings in language. The words are always a form of cover; the real game is always hidden underneath them; however much is said in the course of a play, its heart is in action, which is wordless. Locked into their immediate subtextual interactions, the dramatis personae have no wider orientation, no account to give of themselves: there is a peculiar sense in which they *never say anything*. Something similar is implied by Pinter's famously favourite stage direction, 'pause': it is a repeated suggestion that the truth of the verbal exchanges is to be found by literally reading between the lines. The same ethos is felt again in the playwriting teachers' principle that one should not make a character speak at all without an irresistibly strong reason; in everyday workshop practice this takes the form of injunctions to do less, to cut, to trust the actor to interpret and the audience to infer. A play, it seems, is a peripheral tissue of words wrapped around a core of silence.

At this point, it is not hard to see where this strange taciturnity might come from. As we saw earlier, 'absolute' drama is narrative with no narrator, showing that is not allowed to tell. The charged silence in the middle of it, then, is a trace of the voices that have been silenced in the process of establishing its formal integrity. Drama is monologic not automatically (no use of language is monologic automatically), but because its coherence is sustained by the vigilant suppression of other voices which would cut across or complicate or dialogise it. It is 'pure' drama in the sense that its impurities are actively excluded: it is time to enquire what these might be.

IMPURITIES OF THE THEATRE

To recapitulate: pure drama consists of characters interacting in the medium of spoken dialogue while the dramatist, though omnipresent, is silent. From our account of this form, we can pick out four negative propositions which sustain Bakhtin's contention that drama is inherently monologic.

(1) Not all staged verbal performances count as 'drama' in the strict sense. Some kinds of comic and popular theatre are half outside the category. Drama is wholly monologic only if it excludes these marginal elements.

(2) In a play, each line of dialogue is intelligible as the verbal action of the individual character who utters it. Consequently, the dramatic word is single-voiced; double-voiced speech is impracticable.

(3) Drama is primarily a representation of action, and the dialogue is subordinated to this project. Consequently, different speakers cannot represent different worlds, only different attitudes within the single world that is represented by the play as a whole.

(4) Drama is the opposite of narrative: it is present as opposed to past, enacted as opposed to recounted, showing as opposed to telling. Consequently, dramatic characters, if they are truly dramatic, do not narrate themselves; they behave, and we observe them.

So we see that the category of pure drama is hedged about with exclusions: it is incompatible with the popular and comic stage, with double-voiced speech, with the verbal representation of multiple worlds, and with characters who tell their own story. By taking each of these in turn, we can build up a sense of the dialogic forces that monologic drama labours to suppress.

1. Dialogue and the comic

When I sketched Szondi's model of absolute drama as interpersonal communication, you may have noticed an extraordinary omission: I had nothing to say about actors. There were (fictional) characters talking to each other, and an (absent) author more or less deviously communicating with the audience. But what makes these other transactions possible is the literal encounter in the theatre, when the actor, in role, speaks to the spectators; and this had vanished from the account. If we retrieve the actors from this curious limbo and restore them to the theatre's communicative field, we can immediately see a latent doubleness in *everything* that is said as part of a play. A dramatic line in performance is addressed by the dramatis persona to other dramatis personae, but also, in the same breath, it is addressed by the actor to the audience. It has two speakers and two addressees; 'single-voiced' is exactly what it is not. In other words, one reason drama appears as monologic in Bakhtin is that it is *drama with the theatre left out.*

This omission is not at all an arbitrary piece of absent-mindedness on Bakhtin's part. On the contrary, the disappearance of the actor is essential to the theatrical practice of absolute drama. Its very condition of artistic success, as Szondi points out, has been that the actor should register no separate presence, but merge entirely into the role (Szondi 1987: 8–9). The naturalistic techniques associated with the mid-twentieth-century Actors' Studio in New York, for example, aspired to such truthfulness of physical and vocal gesture that the audience would feel they were witnessing, not anyone's performance, but the character's own unselfconscious behaviour. Correspondingly, the spectators of such theatre sit silently in the dark, and the actors scrupulously avoid meeting their eyes or acknowledging their presence. The audience pretend they are unaware of the actors, and the actors pretend they are unaware of the audience: the whole theatrical relationship is concealed by common consent.

To define this agreement by its opposite, we only need think of the dame in a pantomime. Here the actuality of theatre, the meeting between actor and audience that absolute drama suppresses, comes storming back. The performer talks freely to the spectators and occasionally encourages them to talk back; actor and audience are restored to mutual visibility. And the duality of actor and role, so far from being muted, is positively flaunted because the character is obviously a woman, and the actor representing her is obviously a man. No one supposes what the dame says is the autonomous speech of a female character; rather, 'she' is the *object* – counterfactual fantasy, grotesque mother figure, springboard for jokes – of what the man is doing on the stage. Both women and men are rendered ridiculous by different aspects of the performance; a traditional altercation, a battle of the sexes, is being presented as an internal dialogue by a single actor.

One simple way of saying all that is to describe the pantomime dame as a *parody* of a woman. Bakhtin is interested in parody because it is an elementary paradigm for the representation of another's speech. It consists, essentially, of mockery by imitation; and that means it is a hybrid in which the voice that is being imitated, and the voice that is imitating it, can both be heard distinctly. If the parodied voice is inaudible, nobody will recognise the imitation, and if the parodist's voice is inaudible, nobody will recognise the mockery. There must be both, and in that necessary double-voicedness Bakhtin traces an origin of novelistic discourse (*DI* 74–80). Similarly, parodic acting (the femininity of the dame, but also, say, the badness of a comic villain, or the vanity of a comic fop) needs to articulate both the subjectivity of the 'character', who has intentions and responses within the story, and the objectifying regard of the actor, who understands the character's meaning in the scheme of the play. When the defeated witch in the cinematic pantomime of *The Wizard of Oz* cries 'Who would have thought that some little girl like you could destroy my beautiful wickedness?', the necessary duality is naively, or rather faux-naively, spelt out.

There is a little more to this analogy, though. It is not just that actors as well as writers may engage in parody, but also that parody is *integral* to acting. Imitating another person, consciously reproducing their unconscious mannerisms, always has an edge of mockery; and whereas a writer may or may not be imitating another writer, an actor is an imitator inescapably, as is suggested by the etymology that links 'mimesis' with miming, mimicry and, indeed, pantomime. In other words, a writer who makes fun of other writers by imitating their voices is behaving like an actor. Parody is inherently theatrical. Hence the otherwise surprising theatricality of Bakhtin's conception of the novel's origins: 'The rogue, the clown and the fool were first present in the very cradle of the modern European novel, and there left behind their foolscap and bells among the swaddling clothes' (*DI* 406). On temporary stages at fairs and in marketplaces, the distinctive speech-modes of lawyers or country bumpkins were mockingly copied, or the trickster borrowed the languages of pathos and sincerity for the purposes of deception. Crudely and gaily, the actors showed the embryonic novel how to do heteroglossia.

However, it is hardly accidental that this brief exploration of parody began with a pantomime dame and has ended in a fairground booth. The theatricality that celebrates the reciprocal presence of the actor and the audience does not emerge randomly from theatre in general; it is the distinctive product of popular, comic entertainment. Popular, because it is the theatre of the street and the marketplace that meets its audience face to face in full daylight; and comic, because if the show is funny the audience are not silent. They intervene in the world of the play by laughing, and the performer responds to their world by adjusting the timing of his performance to accommodate their laughter. In short, comic and popular theatres generate kinds of dialogue that seriousness and social exclusiveness tend to silence. In a revealing traditional usage, English theatre refers to forms that are *not* popular or comic entertainment as 'legitimate' drama. It established this legitimacy by distancing itself from a vulgar theatrical immediacy that became, by the same token, illegitimate. Drama does not happen to be monologic, it strove to become so (Weimann 2000).

But although the actor's presence to the audience is so obvious that the legitimate theatre's concealment of it requires great skill, it remains dramatically silent in the sense that the actor, as such, has no lines. Even in comic scenes, the interaction of actor and role is scripted only indirectly, not written out in the substance of the dramatic dialogue but implied in its form. We can see how this works in detail by taking one particular instrument of communication between the stage and the audience: the aside. This is the moment when a character briefly interrupts a dramatic sequence in order to confide in the audience. Shakespeare and his contemporaries used it in all genres, but later dramatists increasingly restricted it to comedy. Asides buttonhole the audience as soliloquies do not, because a soliloquy can just about be interpreted as a character communing with himself, whereas an aside involves switching between external interlocutors in such a focused way that it is impossible to hear it as introspective. Asides are not fragments of inner life but utterances, and if they are not addressed to anyone on the stage, they must be addressed to the audience.

There is a baroque example in George Farquhar's first hit *The Constant Couple* (1699). The wealthy rake-hero, Sir Harry Wildair, is visiting a house where a marriageable young gentlewoman lives with her mother. One of his enemies has told him that the establishment is an upmarket brothel; but the way he introduces himself to the mother is ambiguous enough to secure an interview with the daughter.

LADY DARLING: [*aside to Angelica*] Pray daughter, use him civilly – such matches won't offer every day.
    Exit.

SIR HARRY: [*aside*] O all ye powers of love! an angel! 'Sdeath, what money have I got in my pocket? I can't offer her less than twenty guineas – and by Jupiter she's worth a hundred.

ANGELICA: [*aside*] 'Tis he! the very same! and his person as agreeable as his character of good humour. Pray Heaven his silence proceed from respect.

SIR HARRY: [*aside*] How innocent she looks! How would that modesty adorn virtue, when it makes even vice look so charming! By Heaven, there is

> such a commanding innocence in her looks, that I dare not ask the
> question.
> ANGELICA: [*aside*] Now all the charms of real love and feigned indifference
> assist me to engage his heart, for mine is lost already.
>
> (Farquhar 1995: 2.2.30–44)

Angelica is modest and Sir Harry is nonplussed, so personal
interaction is suspended and they talk separately to the audience
in the pause. The effect is a step back from the dramatic situation: we are listening not to speech acts but to observations
and reflections upon speech acts. But where are the two of
them positioned to make these observations? With each other, in
Lady Darling's reception room, they are incapable of getting a
word out, yet everything they say is fluent and gracefully phrased.
The answer is clearly that they are speaking in the theatre, and
that their syntactic poise is a sign of their easy familiarity, as
actors, with the audience. Thus the unity of the dramatic discourse is split in two: there is no suggestion of identity between
the words spoken on the stage and the words that are supposed to
be spoken in the depicted situation; rather, like narrative prose,
the stage utterances *signify* a sequence of events in the fictional
world, but the theatrical signifier remains separate from the
events. The play does not simply (monologically) show things
being said and done; it tells them, and so articulates an attitude
towards them.

Or rather, several attitudes. Part of the comic point here is that
the encounter which the asides defer has, itself, a double character.
First, it is the most familiar comedy situation of all: the young
principals are smitten with one another, but will they find a way
to say so? Second and more ingeniously, it is the impending
revelation of a ghastly misunderstanding: what is going to
happen when Angelica realises that Sir Harry thinks she is a
prostitute? Because of this doubleness, their dovetailing asides
have a teasing mixture of sameness and difference. On the one
hand they mirror each other: both are silently saying 'I really
fancy you'. On the other hand, Angelica expresses that by saying
she has lost her heart, and Sir Harry by saying she is worth a
hundred guineas. The interplay between these accounts of the

same object creates the conditions for what dramatic dialogue normally excludes: the dialogic *intersection* of discourses.

It is an intersection, not just an opposition, because of the way the two discourses – honourable marriage and prostitution – turn out to be less than completely distinct. Lady Darling's own aside as she leaves them together is inadvertently funny because it could fit comfortably into either. And then the ironies attaching to the principals' respective remarks are morally intricate. When Angelica hopes that Sir Harry's silence proceeds from respect, the line is comic because we know that it proceeds from his difficulty in deciding how much to pay for her. But actually she is not altogether wrong: the blip in his self-assurance does indeed reflect an unexpected sensation of respect. Conversely, when Sir Harry marvels at Angelica's air of innocence, that is another joke, because he means that she looks as if she has no idea what he is there for; and we know that she really does have no idea what he is there for. But in her next line she is plotting ways to 'engage his heart'; so his suggestion that her innocence is a front also contains some truth.

Thus two social languages are brought into complex dialogue with one another: the language of young ladies and suitors, and the language of whores and punters. What makes the dialogue possible is the comic device that uncouples the performers from the actions of the characters and enables them to talk to the audience about what is going on. Including the audience in the conversation has the knock-on effect of opening up the dialogic potential of acting. There is Sir Harry in the drawing room, and there is the actor representing him on the stage, and the playful space between them is full of talk.

2. Double-voiced speech in drama

In a way, the proposition that the dramatic word is single-voiced is an obvious one. Dramatic discourse is distributed among unambiguously differentiated voices which speak one at a time. The internal dialogisation characteristic of the novel is out of the question: it is practically impossible because the various voices emanate from physically distinct persons on the stage, and it is artistically impossible because the intelligibility of the form depends, as we saw in connection with 'good dialogue', on sustaining the illusion that each character is the single origin of what he or she says. But on the other hand it is equally obvious that the dramatic word is not single-voiced at all. One of the things everybody knows about the theatre is that it is full of double-dealing: performing a play means adopting the words, the voice, and the appearance of somebody other than oneself, and, presumably for that reason, dramatic plots often turn on deceptions, pretences, double-bluffs, and substitutions. Dramatic characters typically speak, not out of some originating existential centre, but in the *role* that the action requires them to adopt. The result is, exactly, a kind of double voicing – the simultaneous awareness, audible in the line, of being in role and being outside it. Often this co-existence is itself thematised: for instance, dramatic office-holders from Shakespearean kings to contemporary TV detectives struggle with the tension between their official and their unofficial selves. 'Whose voice are we hearing?' is not always a straightforward question after all.

The great exemplar of this version of dramatic dialogue is Shakespeare. If you open a *Complete Works* at random, you are overwhelmingly likely to turn up a line which, in one way or another, the speaker is delivering 'in role'. Thus, at the end of *Henry VIII*, the Archbishop of Canterbury christens the infant Elizabeth and prophesies the glories of her reign: not only is he speaking in his official capacity as Archbishop, but also he is divinely inspired, so the voice is in a sense that of God (5.4.14–55). In the third act of *The Taming of the Shrew*, when Petruccio marries Katherine, he behaves and speaks with calculated eccentricity in order to disorient Katherine preparatory to her 'taming': he is coolly playing the part of a madman (3.2). In *King Lear*, the king converses with his Fool, who is not a character in the ordinary sense, but a kind of professional entertainer who is never out of costume; as with the Archbishop at the christening, we see him in his official role (1.4.95–188). In the climactic scene of *The Merchant of Venice,* Portia gives her famous speech about the quality of mercy; at the time, she is impersonating a lawyer and taking part in a formal trial (4.1.184–205). Linguists sometimes deploy the concept of a 'canonical speaker': that is, one who is understood to be the origin of a given utterance and can, unlike a messenger or a representative, be regarded as responsible for its content and form. In ordinary conversation canonical speech is taken as the default position; in Shakespeare it is virtually unknown. There is nearly always some complication.

The last of my random samples illustrates the possibilities. Antonio, the merchant of Venice, has defaulted on a loan that was secured by a grotesque bond entitling the Jewish moneylender, Shylock, to a pound of Antonio's flesh. In her character as visiting expert, Portia declares that the bond is good in law, and that the only solution is that Shylock must be merciful. Shylock seizes on the word 'must': 'On what compulsion must I?' The question elicits a speech that schoolchildren used to learn by heart:

> The quality of mercy is not strain'd,
> It droppeth as the gentle rain from heaven
> Upon the place beneath. It is twice blest:
> It blesseth him that gives and him that takes.
> 'Tis mightiest in the mightiest, it becomes
> The throned monarch better than his crown.
> His sceptre shows the force of temporal power,
> The attribute to awe and majesty,
> Wherein doth sit the dread and fear of kings;
> But mercy is above this sceptred sway,
> It is enthroned in the hearts of kings,
> It is an attribute to God himself;
> And earthly power doth then show likest God's
> When mercy seasons justice. Therefore, Jew,
> Though justice be thy plea, consider this,
> That in the course of justice, none of us
> Should see salvation. We do pray for mercy,
> And that same prayer should teach us all to render
> The deeds of mercy. I have spoke thus much
> To mitigate the justice of thy plea,
> Which if thou follow, this strict court of Venice
> Must needs give sentence 'gainst the merchant there.

(4.1.184–205)

In the immediate context of the court, the last few lines of this speech place it as a sort of procedural requirement. The justice of Shylock's claim is clear, but the extraordinary circumstances constitute a case for mercy, and so the doctor of laws has a duty to make sure that it is put. He therefore delivers a set-piece speech, highly competent and conventional, devoted to the proposition that mercy is a finer thing than justice. The 'voice' at this level is that of the lawyer Portia is pretending to be, doing his best, professionally but unsuccessfully, to persuade Shylock to change his mind.

But this speaker is not only a legal functionary: he is also a mystery. He is a sexually ambiguous stranger; no-one knows him, and the audience realise that he is a fiction. He arrives from Padua when the hearing has already begun; he is a messenger from a lawyer named Bellario, but it is not quite clear whether he is to make his own judgment in the case, or is merely the bearer of Bellario's opinion. In any case, he immediately takes over the entire conduct of the court: it seems not to occur to the Duke of Venice or anyone else to question his authority. In short, this is a 'messenger' in a quasi-religious sense: an angel coming from another world to untie the bonds in which 'earthly power' has become entangled. This is voiced in the central sequence of the speech, when the praise of mercy ascends through the image of kingship to 'God himself'. The grandeur of the sentence carries it away from its immediate argumentative purpose into a register which is closer to prophetic than forensic. Bellario is not a character in the play, only the name of an offstage source of wisdom and truth: these lines are spoken by the emissary of this unseen authority, the bringer of his gifts.

There is also a third element in the voicing of the speech. In the plot, there is no hope of persuading Shylock to be merciful: he makes it brutally clear that he is not listening. Antonio will eventually be saved not by pleas for mercy but by a legal manoeuvre: Portia will point out that although the bond entitles Shylock to cut off his pound of flesh, it does not permit him to shed any blood while doing so, and this will force Shylock to give up his claim. So the ostensible purpose of the 'mercy' speech is illusory: it is not possible to change Shylock's mind, and it is not necessary either. Rather, the real point of the speech, delivered while Portia is still holding her ace in her sleeve, is that it gives Shylock the opportunity to dig himself into a deeper hole. She presses him again and again with alternatives to the murderous implementation of the bond: he could listen to more pleading; he could be merciful; he could take the money; he could at least have surgeons in attendance. These sound to him, and to the audience, like appeals from weakness, but actually they are offers from strength, his last chances to mitigate the judgment that is about to drop upon him. He rejects them all, and the words which he imagines are confirming his enemy's fate are in fact sealing his own. The speech plays its part in this charade of self-incrimination. It ensures that when Shylock refuses to show mercy, it is with a full understanding of what it is.

So 'The quality of mercy ... ' is not only a piece of legal rhetoric and a manifestation of divine truth, it is also a trick. The speaker at this third level is neither a lawyer nor an angel, but the heroine of a comedy, outwitting the villain. As such, she is speaking playfully. Not frivolously (it is a serious game), but in the knowledge that the developing dialogue, which the other participants suppose to be a matter of life and death, is really only the *appearance* of a matter of life and death: in other words, a play. In that voice, the sequence about mercy as an attribute to God himself sounds less like a sacred revelation and more like an improvised hyperbole. It is as if the speech is framed by a gesture that says 'let's try this'. What Portia says may be true, but she is not saying it *because* it is true; she is saying it to see what Shylock will say in response.

The famous words, then, are commanded by three separable intentions, voiced for three speakers who play fluidly against one another because all are contained in the same character. The declaration that dramatic speech has to be single-voiced turns out to have been based on a simplistic conception of drama. The multiplication of roles has the effect of freeing the word from an inescapable connection with any one of them: the speech appears as a sort of verbal artefact, serving several different communicative intentions but standing apart from them all. The force of this suspension becomes apparent when the charade ends and Shylock is defeated. A torrent of judgment breaks over him: he loses his case, the winners joyfully taunt him, he is immediately convicted of plotting the death of a Venetian citizen, his wealth and his life are forfeit to the state, and these penalties are remitted only on the basis that he converts to Christianity. The comedy is enjoying the moment when the villain gets his just desserts, and Portia, still in her role as exponent of the law, insists that 'the Jew shall have all justice' (4.1.321). What is the relationship between this fierce triumph of the juvenile leads and the gentle praise of mercy that one of them recently delivered? Insofar as the speech was part of a game, they fit together without strain: the game is won now, and it is appropriate to celebrate the victory. But insofar as it was the enunciation of a general truth transcending the action, it hovers over the humiliation of 'the Jew' with uneasy irony. Portia is not wholly in control of the eloquence that is wrung from her by her fantastical situation; she is drawn into an unresolved argument with herself. The dramatic character does not after all render the discourse single-voiced; rather, it is itself dialogised.

3. Multiple worlds

The salience of Shakespeare as an example of dramatic 'impurity' is not accidental. Historically, he was writing for a theatre *before* the hegemony of pure drama, while at the same time the extra-ordinary persistence of his plays on the stage has meant that the memory of a pre-modern theatricality, actor-oriented and double-voiced, is never quite lost. An exceptionally straightforward example of this is provided by the question of scene-setting. According to Szondi, the paradigmatic setting of 'absolute' drama is the picture-frame stage: its marked-off visual plenitude connotes the self-complete system of the play's interpersonal relationships, absolutely separate from the auditorium on the other side of the frame (Szondi 1987: 8). This is the stage of which Bakhtin says, 'it cannot contain multiple worlds: it permits only one, and not several, systems of measurement' (*PDP* 34). The play's different speakers may have radically different ideas about things, but they all have them in the same context: we can see that just by looking at them. With Shakespeare's plays, however, this closure is uncertain because, as everyone knows, many of them were first performed on a thrust stage with no scenery. In this context, the spectators need the spoken word to tell them what they are supposed to be seeing, and this gives the dialogue a quasi-performative power: as things are said to be, so they are.

This world-creating word is a well-worn theme in the praise of Shakespeare's genius. He is said to make up for his theatre's lack of visual effects by the vividness of his verbal scene-painting. But to put it like that is to simplify what is going on. Let us look at a textbook example, again from *Macbeth*. It is when King Duncan and his courtiers, who have come to stay at Macbeth's castle, are waiting at the entrance for somebody to welcome them.

DUNCAN: This castle hath a pleasant seat, the air
    Nimbly and sweetly recommends itself
    Unto our gentle senses.
BANQUO: This guest of summer,
    The temple-haunting marlet, does approve,
    By his loved mansionry, that the heaven's breath
    Smells wooingly here; no jutty, frieze,
    Buttress, nor coign of vantage, but this bird
    Hath made his pendant bed and procreant cradle.
    Where they most breed and haunt, I have observ'd
    The air is delicate.

(1.6. 1–10)

Certainly the realisation of place here is wonderfully skilful. The situation makes it natural for the visitors to say something about the castle, and then Banquo's observation about the nesting birds prompts a fairly detailed inspection, inviting the actor to point physically at the jutties, friezes, and buttresses of an imaginary building. The location is conjured into existence by vivid and subtle deixis.

Yet 'scene-painting' is an inadequate term for what this exchange is doing. For one thing, it is not describing the castle's appearance. The whole conversation is about the air: Duncan says it is sweet, and Banquo confirms his impression with a theory that 'marlets' (swifts) prefer to nest in places where the air is good. So the words are not substituting for the supposedly missing scenery, but evoking something that scenery could not portray anyway. The description is not visual, scarcely even sensory. More than anything else, it is about a feeling: it represents the castle as a place of love. The air 'sweetly recommends itself', its 'breath smells wooingly'; the bird is a 'guest', its nesting here is 'loved', and the nest itself is a 'procreant cradle'. The observed world is saturated in the observer's emotions and associations. These associations are not so much personal as socially appropriate: this is how a castle *ought* to seem to honoured guests who are about to experience its hospitality. Later in the short scene, Duncan will speak explicitly about Macbeth's love for him and his for Macbeth. Here, Macbeth's castle is bathed in the mild radiance of that mutuality.

The exchange is therefore a reply to Lady Macbeth's anticipation of exactly this moment. For her, it is very differently illuminated by her intention to murder the king:

> The raven himself is hoarse
> That croaks the fatal entrance of Duncan
> Under my battlements.

(1.5. 38–40)

Instead of the amorous marlet, the ominous raven; instead of heaven's breath, hoarse croaking; instead of the accommodating nesting places, menacing 'battlements'. Thus one particular moment in the story – the king's arrival at Macbeth's castle – is 'done' in two antithetic languages, one oriented towards life and the other towards death. Moreover, either description can claim to be the true one. Banquo's account gives the event as it should properly be, and as it actually does appear; it makes Lady Macbeth's version seem like a travesty. But her account presages what is really going to happen; it makes Banquo's version seem like a fool's paradise. Two arrivals, at two castles, are in play.

So it is not the case that the play is bound to bring its different verbally generated 'worlds' to a single measure. Since the stage is no more than a potential world until its nature is specified by the quasi-performative power of the word, it is possible for a play to offer more than one specification, and for the specifications to be incompatible. We therefore have the conditions that Bakhtin thought inconsistent with the logic of drama:

> The weakening or destruction of a monologic context occurs only when there is a coming together of two utterances equally and directly oriented toward a referential object. Two discourses equally and directly oriented toward a referential object within the limits of a single context cannot exist side by side without intersecting dialogically. ... Two equally weighted discourses on one and the same theme, once having come together, must inevitably orient themselves to one another.
>
> (*PDP* 188–89)

In this way, Shakespearean theatre institutes a dialogue not merely of objectified speakers, but of 'world-making' *discourses*.

4. Self-narration

Our fourth and final exclusion was narrative. Pure drama shows, in the present; telling, in the past, is supposedly undramatic. Of course, narrative speeches are common, even normal, in classical plays. At the end of the comedy, the old nurse tells the story that explains who the hero really is; at the end of the tragedy, the messenger comes on to report the terrible catastrophe that has just taken place offstage. But these devices do not trouble the mutually exclusive opposition of narrative and drama. On the contrary, they secure it: by consigning physically and temporally heterogeneous events to a merely described realm beyond the boundaries of the play, they guarantee the consistency and self-presence of the dramatic world itself. *That* happened last summer or in another town, so we need to be told about it; *this* does not need to be narrated because it is happening in front of us.

But that opposition does not really give us the measure of a speech like this one from the opening of Chekhov's *Three Sisters* (1904):

> It's warm today. We can have the windows wide. The birch trees aren't out yet, though. Father got his brigade and left Moscow with us

eleven years ago, and I well remember what Moscow was like at this time of year, at the beginning of May. Everything would be in blossom already, everything would be warm, everything would be awash with sunshine. Eleven years have gone by, but I remember it all as if it were yesterday. Oh God, I woke up this morning, I saw the light flooding in, I saw the spring, and I felt such a great surge of joy, such a passionate longing for home.

(Chekhov 1983: 2)

Olga is not simply supplementing the present with a report on a specified past. Times and places flow into one another as she speaks: this spring as well as spring in Moscow 11 years ago; early this morning as well as now. Memory and sensation form a unity of impression that overwhelms the boundary between describing and dramatising. She is not interacting with anyone particularly, and it is difficult to resolve what she says into a 'speech act'. (For example, what are the first three or four sentences of her speech doing? Her only interlocutors are her sisters, who do not need to be told any of these things.) Rather, she is narrating herself, constructing not 'the' world of the play but *her* world, where the external 'flood' of sunlight overlaps with the inner 'surge' of her joy, inextricably mixed up with nostalgia and the fact that she is 28. Her words, then, are not simply interactive behaviour for the audience to observe, but also constitute her account of who she is and how she experiences her life. It is as if the silence of pure drama has been broken: a woman is talking to us.

This is not a stroke of sheer innovation on Chekhov's part. Once again, the dramatic impurity is a renewal of a performing convention older and more universal than the canon it violates. It is almost a foundational act, in sacred theatre, in folk plays, in courtly masques, that a costumed figure presents himself to the audience and makes a speech explaining who he is. Sometimes, indeed, this gesture of self-presentation dominates the show, so that the main action is not any kind of story, but just the festive, estranging encounter between the imaginary being and the real crowd. In John Skelton's play *Magnyfycence* (c. 1520), for example, the monarchical figure of the title is assailed by a flock of vices with extravagant names like Cloaked Collusion, Courtly Abusion, and Crafty Conveyance. They have interactive scenes, but these are interrupted at regular intervals so that each vice can introduce itself in a lengthy monologue; it is in these speeches that Skelton writes with the greatest poetic freedom and energy. An audience that regarded them as mere exposition, preparatory to the action, would go mad with impatience. The point is to *stage* the vices, and the solo performance is one way of doing that, no doubt less 'dramatic' than involving them in a plot, but not less theatrical.

Self-narration is ancient, then, but it is not archaic. Both the lyricism of *Three Sisters* and the solo virtuosity of *Magnyfycence* point to what in a way is the most obvious home of all for such expression: musical theatre. Musical plays afford their characters two radically different kinds of voice: when they speak, they interact with each other as in drama; when they sing, even if the words of the song are notionally addressed to another character, the statement outgrows the fictional occasion and addresses itself to to the audience. Almost any example would exhibit this familiar but logically complex shift; I shall look at one classic, *Pal Joey*.

This Rodgers and Hart musical aspired, as it were, to the status of drama. When it was first staged, in 1940, it was normal for the books of musicals to be fairly silly and formulaic, explicitly vehicles for the stars, the songs, and the dancing. This one, by John O'Hara, makes a move away from the formula and towards the moral seriousness and psychological realism associated with 'legitimate' drama. Both the seriousness and the realism are diluted in the film version of 1957, but the tension between different theatrical modes can still be felt. Joey, a hard-bitten and unsuccessful night-club MC, has an affair with a wealthy married woman named Mrs Simpson who falls for his cock-eyed mixture of stylishness and vulgarity. She comes up with the capital for him to have his own club, and the story follows the progress of their relationship to its inevitably bitter end.

The dramatic writing of this action is what Bakhtin calls 'objectifying'. We are shown how Mrs Simpson's infatuation comes out of her boredom, her *nostalgie de la boue*, her unreflective assumption that she can get what she wants by paying for it; we see the contradictions in which Joey is trapped, as his attempts to gatecrash good society expose his ignorance of it, and his plan to become a proud owner leads to his being humiliatingly owned. The dialogue is as it were a series of symptoms which the audience observes; the index of the drama's seriousness is the characters' moral knowability; a monologic framework is clamped firmly round their interaction. However, when Mrs Simpson falls in love with Joey she sings the show's best known song, 'Bewitched, Bothered and Bewildered'. The tune is a sinuous ballad which became a jazz standard almost at once, and the lyric has a matching verbal virtuosity:

> I'm wild again,
> Beguiled again,
> A simpering, whimpering child again—
> Bewitched, bothered and bewildered am I ...
>
> A pill he is,
> But still he is
> All mine, and I'll keep him until he is
> Bewitched, bothered and bewildered like me.
>
> (Gottlieb and Kimball 2000: 196–97)

Here, audible all at once, is the 'voice of another', literally so in the film, since the actress, Rita Hayworth, is noticeably over-dubbed with the voice of a singer, Jo Ann Greer. Its effect is to unlock the monologism of the drama. Not that the song reveals psychological nuances the dialogue concealed, or that the relationship is any less stereotypical than it was before. Rather, the change is in the situation of the performer. As an actor in the play she was of course performing, but the performance was masked as behaviour, and the appropriate reaction of the audience was to watch and judge the character interacting with those around her. Now, the fact that she is performing is explicit, flaunted in the lush strings, the conspicuously witty rhymes, the piquant combination of confessed helplessness and relaxed self-awareness. Suddenly we are in the presence, not of the limited and selfish woman of the story, but of a star doing a big number, playing the crowd, confiding in it, commanding its emotions, presenting a universal image of beauty and glamour and sexual delight. In short, the code of drama gives way to the code of show-business, and that gives 'Mrs Simpson' the authority to stop being an object within the story and flood the theatre with subjectivity. The dramatic principle that characters are definingly unaware, that their words have no power to confer meaning on their experiences, has been overturned.

These three examples – Olga, Crafty Conveyance, and Mrs Simpson – were formed within fundamentally different conventions of representation. Between them, then, they suggest that this phenomenon is found right across the theatre. It is a sort of lyric uprising against the hegemony of drama, resisting its rule of silence, giving the actor words. Working through the examples has turned up one more thing too: as it happens, all three are characterised by radical ambivalence. Olga's speech registers joy and unbearable loss in the same breath. Skelton's vices are satiric monsters boasting about their badness, and so combining affirmation and denunciation in the same words. 'Bewitched, Bothered and Bewildered' expresses a feeling of triumphant fulfilment through a vocabulary of helplessness and confusion. These ambivalences do *not* intimate divided feelings on the part of the characters: both Olga and Mrs Simpson project a radiant singleness of mood, and the vices belong to a convention that precludes moral uncertainty. Rather, what produces the contradictory discourses is the way that each speaker's world is articulated from the inside and the outside at the same time. In being given the power to narrate herself, the theatrical figure is split in two – the narrator and the hero of the narrative, the one who describes and the one who acts. The always implicit duality of the actor finds explicit dramatic form, and the outcome is a dialogic language of the stage.

EPIC THEATRE

The principle that the actor is two-fold is central to one of the most deliberate modern attempts to redefine European drama: the project of epic theatre. Its exponent, the playwright and director Bertolt Brecht (1898–1956), insisted on this duality in several different theoretical texts, including the essay 'The Street Scene'.

This piece supposes that there has been an accident in the street, and that a bystander who witnessed it explains what happened by demonstrating, for example, where the driver and the victim were in relation to each other, how they were behaving, what movements he saw them make. Brecht proposes a new kind of theatre which would derive all its significant principles from this impromptu street-corner enactment – its basis in observation, its intention to be useful, its concentration on practical interaction rather than inner feeling, and also this:

> One essential element of the street scene lies in the natural attitude adopted by the demonstrator, which is two-fold; he is always taking two situations into account. He behaves naturally as a demonstrator, and he lets the subject of the demonstration behave naturally too. He never forgets, nor does he allow it to be forgotten, that he is not the subject but the demonstrator. That is to say, what the audience sees is not a fusion between demonstrator and subject, not some third, independent, uncontradictory entity with isolated features of (a) demonstrator and (b) subject, such as the orthodox theatre puts before us in its productions. The feelings and opinions of demonstrator and demonstrated are not merged into one.
>
> (Brecht 1964: 125)

That is to say that the relationship between 'demonstrator and demonstrated', the person who is showing the accident and the person who was involved in it, takes the form of a dialogue. It is not only that the demonstrator was watching, and therefore may have noticed aspects of the driver's behaviour that he was not himself aware of; it is also that the demonstrator has opinions about who is responsible for the accident and how it could have been avoided. These opinions shape the representation: the demonstrator highlights the moments that seem to him decisive, perhaps repeating them or commenting on them directly, while if on the other hand there are details which in his view have no bearing on the accident, he merely sketches them, or leaves them out altogether. The little 'play' about the accident, then, has the structure of an argument, not the structure of an accident. If the performance were so vivid that the spectators felt as if they were actually experiencing a car crash, then it would fail to carry out its communicative purpose, because the force of the event would silence the conversation about it.

Most obviously, this is a model for performance: Brecht is urging actors to modify their technique in such a way that they no longer lose themselves in the characters they play. However, the man on the corner not only performs his account of the incident but also devises it; he stands for the dramatist as well as the actor. The allegorical scope of the street scene goes well beyond its deliberately unpretentious vehicle: the 'demonstrator' denotes the whole practice of theatre, and the street accident stands for much larger social and historical mishaps. The essay was probably written in 1938. In 1939 European civilisation skidded off the road and injured several pedestrians; by the end of the year Brecht had the first draft of his roadside demonstration, *Mother Courage and her Children*.

During the German religious wars of the seventeenth century, Mother Courage supports herself and her children by supplying food and clothing to the contending armies. As well as sustaining the family the war destroys it: by the end of the play all three children have been killed, and the mother is left alone with her now largely futile business. The story is simple, but the question of how to understand it is oddly intractable. On the one hand, the play is an endlessly taught classic, and anyone who has ever studied it knows it is about Mother Courage's failure to learn from her experience. She goes along with the war in every sense, crossing countries to keep up with it and working tirelessly to supply its material needs. She is profoundly complicit with its workings; this complicity brings death to her children; but even when the last and most innocent of them has been lost, she is still incapable of revoking her devil's bargain. She is a kind of monster, an unforgettable image (staged in the ruins of Berlin in 1948) of a population embracing war out of avarice and stupidity. On the other hand, anyone who has ever seen the play knows that Mother Courage is a shamelessly crowd-pleasing star role. Written for Brecht's wife Helene Weigel, and dominating almost every scene, the character is hard-working, funny, brave, selfless, shrewd, and, in the painful ironies surrounding the children's deaths, a figure of extreme pathos. Students are sometimes told that Brecht intended Mother Courage to be 'unsympathetic', as if he had made her the heroine in a fit of absent-mindedness: this is not plausible.

The solution to the dilemma is found in the street scene. The expectation that Mother Courage should be unsympathetic if she exemplifies something to which the dramatist is opposed, or, conversely, that if she is likeable it follows that she has the dramatist's approval, is based on the assumption that she is, precisely, 'a fusion between demonstrator and subject', a 'third, independent, uncontradictory entity' in which the feelings and opinions of demonstrator and demonstrated are 'merged into one'. Such an entity would presumably be a compromise between her folly and her intelligence, her generosity and her greed: a 'complex character' who is partly sympathetic and partly not. By blocking its formation, and insisting instead on the separate identities of 'demonstrator and demonstrated', the show releases *both* from the need to compromise. The 'demonstrated', Mother Courage, is free to claim the audience's sympathy with all the eloquence and charm that the artists can afford her, while on the other hand the *mise en scène*, working through songs, interlocutors, significant juxtapositions, narrative ironies, and choric commentary, as well as the sceptical intelligence of the actor herself, functions as the 'demonstrator', arguing remorselessly that this wonderful woman is lethally wrong about everything of importance in her life. The coherence of the representation consists not in unification, but in the dialogue of unmerged voices, the argument between the dangerous driver and the critical bystander.

Thus, exactly contemporary with Bakhtin's essays on novelistic discourse, we have a fully and consciously worked out instance of dialogised dramatic speech. In a way, Brecht's exception proves Bakhtin's rule. In order to unlock the mystical unity of the dramatic character, and rediscover the inherent dialogic potential of acting, it was apparently necessary to invent a whole new model of theatre, which suggests that the old one was indeed confined within the monologic framework Bakhtin thought inescapable. After all, Brecht's chosen brand name, 'epic theatre', is a deliberate challenge to what we have seen is the constitutive opposition between drama and narrative. What supposedly distinguishes epic from dramatic form – the extension of time and place beyond the immediate present, the switching between the differently oriented voices of narrator and hero – is exactly what Brecht wanted for the theatre. In other words he *shared* Bakhtin's implicit assessment of the limitations of drama; it is just that his response was to try and change the nature of drama so as not to get stuck with them.

Of course, this was never a question of absolute innovation. We have seen at some length that the theatre, at its margins or in its earlier history, was already alive with dialogic forces. Cross-dressing, parody, burlesque, direct address to the audience, Shakespearean role-playing, travestied trials and ceremonies, self-narration, musical numbers: practically all of the elements I noted in my survey of theatrical 'impurities' are dusted off and re-used somewhere in Brecht's plays. The defining task of 'epic' theatre, you might say, was to gather up and systematise everything in theatrical tradition that contradicted the monologic closure of the 'dramatic'. Conceptually the two categories do indeed have this binary relation. It is not coincidental, for instance, that Peter Szondi's essay about 'absolute drama' appeared in 1956, when Brecht's European reputation was at its highest. It was because the canons of drama had been powerfully and consciously transgressed that it was possible for criticism to identify them.

Ultimately, though, Brecht's interests were not of this formal kind. His main reason for choosing the street scene as a model is not that it rediscovers the suppressed duality of actor and role; it is that it suggests a theatre immersed in the affairs of the society where it finds itself. The demonstrator on the street corner is taking part in a discussion that has practical consequences: was the accident avoidable? is the victim entitled to compensation? Of course the professional theatre deals with wider and more profound questions than that; but Brecht is demanding that it should do so in the same sociable spirit. In other words, he is recommending the street scene not only as a paradigm for the theatre, but also as a living source. The art of drama needs to stay in touch with:

Das alltägliche, tausendfache und ruhmlose
Aber so sehr lebendige, irdische, aus dem Zusammenleben
Der Menschen gespeiste Theater, das auf der Straße sich abspielt.

('Über Alltägliches Theater', Brecht 1967: 766)

(The everyday, thousandfold, unsung
But intensely living, earthly theatre, which is fed from people's
Living together, and whose stage is the street.)

This praises the theatre, or at least a possible theatre, in terms that echo Bakhtin's praise of the novel: that it is nourished by its roots in living social heteroglossia. If it is dialogic, that is not finally because of its own internal structures, but because it is itself participating in the unending conversation that is *das Zusammenleben der Menschen*. Brecht's actor is an artist not as opposed to a social being but *as* a social being, speaking in carefully practised ways to his fellow citizens in the auditorium. What everything depends on, in that case, is not the dialogue in the play, but the dialogue the play is in.

4

DIALOGUE IN LITERARY STUDIES

In a recent introduction to the subject of sexuality in Shakespeare, the critic and cultural historian Bruce R. Smith reflects on the fact that the words 'sexual' and 'sexuality' were unknown to Shakespeare, since they came into existence only in the course of the nineteenth century (Smith 2003: 431–33). For the forces and emotions that are unmistakably at work in *Othello* or *Measure For Measure*, early modern English had a different repertoire of terms: 'passion', 'appetite', 'sense'. These are not simply ancient synonyms for the modern word: they are the names of concepts that divide the realm of experience up in a radically different way, and imply a different theory of how human beings work. That is, to speak of sexuality in Shakespeare is to introduce not only an alien word but an alien *meaning*: it involves a kind of anachronism.

However, Smith immediately adds that the anachronism is inescapable. Actors, audiences, readers, and critics must experience the plays within the frames of reference they actually inhabit: after Freud, after Fanon, after Foucault, it would be both impossible and pointless to view Othello solely in the light of the psychic and physiological knowledge of the Renaissance.

> What is needed is a strategy that deploys the term *sexuality* with full awareness of its present-day specificity, that recognizes the difference of bodily experience in the past from what it is today, and that bridges the gap between the two by putting past and present into dialogue.
>
> (433)

Smith's invocation of 'dialogue' here is quite typical of contemporary literary criticism: the term seems to name the relationship with the writings of the past that scholars would like to have. He is equally representative, though, in identifying a 'need' for a 'strategy' to set up such a dialogue, implying that its establishment is neither easy nor unopposed. The dialogue of past and present is not something that just happens; it has to be devised.

This final chapter, then, will consider dialogue as part of the conceptual repertoire of literary studies itself. It will explore the conditions of possibility of the wished-for dialogue of past and present, and show how this particular project emerges from the nature of the discipline. First of all, let us look at the question negatively: what makes it *difficult* to converse with the past?

THE GO-BETWEEN

'The past is a foreign country: they do things differently there' (Hartley 1958: 7). The opening sentence of L.P. Hartley's novel *The Go-Between*, first published in 1953, is much quoted because it encapsulates something people intuitively feel to be true. Time is experienced as a widening gulf on whose farther shore live people quite different from ourselves. History, in that case, is the study of these foreign countries, and specifically of their foreignness: what constitutes a historical 'period' is that it is radically different from now. Although this experience is widely shared, it does not quite follow that it is inevitable. In the very startlingness of Hartley's formulation there is a tacit suggestion that things could or even should be different: that the years between ought to connect us to the past rather than separating us from it; that we could enjoy a world in common with our ancestors through descent and inheritance; that the past might strike us not as a foreign country but precisely as home.

The aphorism itself, after all, is not quite the universally acknowledged truth that its positioning makes it resemble. The next sentence attaches it to Hartley's narrator, Leo, a man in his sixties who has chanced to find a diary which he kept in the year 1900, when he was 13, and which he has not opened since. It soon transpires that the closed book is an emblem of repression: the events of that summer culminated in a traumatic moment which the pubescent boy buried so deeply as to blight, sexually and emotionally, the adult life over which he now looks back. The years between, then, do literally appear to the reader as barren time. The half-century between event and recollection contains no mediation or development, no material capable of carrying meaning, only the widening gulf. But this emptiness is not normal; the colon that breaks the opening sentence in two is, as it turns out, a mark of psychic damage. The past is alien, not always and of itself, but because the one who remembers is alienated.

The psychological story is overlaid with a historical one. The fact that the year was 1900 is much insisted upon: Leo was boyishly excited by it, and evokes it as filled with the glamour and promise of the new century, a promise that is of course an ironic memory by the time he is recalling it in 1952. Moreover, the story of the summer turns on class distinctions that are expressly part of the different way the Victorians 'do things'. It takes place at Brandham Hall, a rural mansion owned by an aristocrat and let to a merchant banker; the banker's daughter is engaged to the aristocrat, thus enacting the classic English harmonisation of money and rank. The eventual trauma is connected with the young Leo's being the innocent 'go-between' in an affair between the daughter and a local farmer, a heavily signalled violation of the class boundaries that the life of the Hall is designed to police. When Leo, moved by his memories, returns to the place in 1952, the Hall is occupied by a girls' school, and the daughter is living in what used to be the cottage occupied by her nanny. Her aristocratic husband is long dead, and her son was killed in the Second World War. So Leo's personal loss of connectedness with his past is matched by the familiar story of the decline of the English country house, in which modern war and modern economics disrupt the continuity of inherited privilege. All this appears to have happened during Leo's lifetime of denial, as if he had closed his eyes after tea on the lawn in 1900, and opened them again in 1952 to find that everything had vanished. The book shares a structure of feeling with Evelyn Waugh's *Brideshead Revisited* (1945), which deploys a similar retrospective narrative frame. A kind of fast-forward effect gives the ending of the mythic pre-war summer the force of a shock.

The novel heightens this rhetoric still further by giving the remembered time a serio-comic air of magic. The portentous diary is decorated with the signs of the zodiac, and Leo, already associated with them by his name, harnesses their power to perform spells. It is a freak summer, the temperature rising daily to improbable heights, and the boy maintains something between a belief and a game that his own powers are driving it up. The inhabitants of the Hall are the immortals, and as the go-between Leo is Mercury, the messenger of the Gods (as well as the element in the thermometer). The *differentness* of the past is dramatised by this quasi-supernatural character. It is not a particularly happy place: like most pantheons, it is marked by a good deal of cruelty and fear. But it is alive with invisible energies. Here too, the atmosphere seems generic rather than unique: the novel's moment in the 1950s is also that of children's classics like Mary Norton's *The Borrowers* (1952) and Philippa Pearce's *Tom's Midnight Garden* (1958), which also stage the retrieval, as magic, of a country house past.

We could loosely call this a *post-war* structure. The magical connection with the past is in effect an image of historical rupture: that era is so completely departed that only a spell can raise it. The past is not a lost home; too much has changed for that; it is a foreign country, an enchanted place which we see by night or in tantalising fragments. In other words, Leo's repression is resonant because it is emblematic of a severed continuity. Both the novel and the famous sentiment with which it begins register the disorienting remoteness of the past, not as a universal experience, but as the aftermath of a disaster. We would like to speak with these people, to resume the conversation, but we cannot make a connection; Mercury, the little god who carries messages, has failed. What has defeated him, in some ultimate sense, is modernity.

UNDERSTANDING AS DIALOGUE

One could almost say that *Truth and Method*, the magnum opus of the philosopher Hans-Georg Gadamer (1900–2002), is designed to prove that Hartley's casual aphorism is false: that on the contrary we *do* belong to the same country, and speak the same language, as the writings of the past. *Truth and Method* was published in German in 1960 and first translated into English in 1975. Its subject is hermeneutics, that is, the theory and method of the interpretation of texts. It is an intricate book whose argument can be summarised in several different ways, depending on the interests of the summariser. Our interests prompt one particular and selective formula: Gadamer maintains that understanding has the character of a dialogue.

One problem with this bald statement of the idea is that both 'understanding' and 'dialogue' are axiomatically good things. Like creativity, or empathy, they are regarded as valuable qualities in every kind of joint enterprise, from marriages to hedge funds; it is hard to imagine an opponent of understanding and dialogue who would not be equally opposed to human life in general. As a result, associating them with each other sounds at first like a simple piety, as if we were being told that one should develop good listening skills and respect the other person's point of view. It helps us to separate Gadamer's thought from these platitudes if we begin by imagining its contrary. How might it be rationally maintained that understanding does *not* have the character of a dialogue?

Gadamer's answer to that question, which underlies his whole enquiry, is that Western thought since the Enlightenment has been dominated by what is, exactly, a non-dialogic model of understanding: namely, that of natural science. At the heart of this model is the idea of observation. A mental subject apprehends a physical object, and, by repeatedly manipulating it, recontextualising it and noting its regularities, acquires an incremental power to determine its origins and predict its future. This power can reasonably be termed 'understanding': the subject is what understands, the object is what is understood, and the monument of the process is the utterly unprecedented practical knowledge of nature achieved by such means over the past two or three centuries. Here, then, is a method whose conception of understanding bears no relation to dialogue; here, understanding means understanding an *object* that remains itself silent, thing-like, known or merely not yet known. The method's achievements and authority are so undeniable as to put pressure on disciplines outside the sphere of natural science, and in particular on what Gadamer's translators call the 'human sciences': the study of human society and culture, centrally including history. Is the objective model universal? Are historians and anthropologists and philologists pursuing the same kind of understanding as natural scientists, albeit with less exact and stable data? Or are scholars in the humanities engaged in something radically different, with a different conception, from the start, of what it means to understand something? It is at this point that the idea of dialogue stops being a platitude.

The humanities, after all, are by definition the study not of the inanimate world but of human meanings, whose principal medium is language. The 'data' consist not of observations but of utterances; so the relevant model is not the way we understand objects, but the way we understand what people say to us. As a 'human scientist', I work differently from a natural scientist because I am dealing right from the beginning with someone else's intention, which I cannot just override or assimilate to my own; I have to 'take in', as we say, what the other person is saying, I have to *get* what they mean. Gadamer describes this convergence by equating *understanding* with *coming to an understanding* – in other words, the effort to understand what the other person is saying is, in the same breath, an effort to reach agreement with them (180). This argument is easier to make in German, because of the close connection between the words corresponding to 'understanding' (*Verständnis*) and 'agreement' (*Einverständnis*). But it is not really untranslatable: in English, in legal or commercial contexts for example, there is not much difference between an 'understanding' and an 'agreement'. The mechanism of the attempt is that of 'the art of conversation'. Through 'argument, question and answer, objection and refutation', we work towards a shared perception of the matter in hand (181); agreement may not be reached, of course, but in any case the attempt to reach it is what gives shape to the interaction. In one word, understanding a verbal communication, even a written one, entails conducting a dialogue with it.

This conception of understanding has some surprising consequences. One of them concerns the role of what Gadamer, following earlier hermeneutic writers, calls 'fore-meaning' (269–71). The idea is that as you try to understand a text, you are constantly projecting versions of its unity, of what the whole thing will turn out to mean. If one of these fore-meanings collides with something in the text that is incompatible with it, then you are compelled to abandon it and come up with another version that accommodates the newly apprehended element. And so on: this repeated shuttling between projection and disconfirmation is one way of describing the dialogue Gadamer takes understanding to be. But he adds that the fore-meanings are not simply imperfect logical deductions from the text. They are also *your* meanings, shaped and populated by everything you suppose you already know about the subject of the text and the language in which it is written. The dialogue, then, does not only consist of questions and answers about the text and its meaning; it is also about your own prior assumptions, so that *'The hermeneutic task becomes of itself a questioning of things'* (271 – Gadamer's italics). It is by virtue of putting a strain on your sense of the world that a text makes itself understood.

It follows that there are two ways of being a bad reader. The first way is to block the text's corrections of your fore-meanings by sticking to your preconceptions and ignoring whatever doesn't fit them: the failure of understanding here is obvious and not very interesting. The second way of being a bad reader, which interests Gadamer much more, is to try and approach the text with an entirely open mind. In this case, you aim to make yourself into a neutral recipient of its meanings, divesting yourself of every prior assumption that might get in the way. The objection to this is not so much that it cannot be achieved (even if neutrality is unattainable, striving towards it might still be a valid method); it is rather that since understanding is a function of the interaction between the text's meanings and the reader's preconceptions, suppressing the latter will disable the whole process. If the first bad reader wrecked the dialogue by refusing to hear the other voice, the second one wrecks the same dialogue, equally effectively, by refusing to volunteer anything himself. Hermeneutically speaking, he has failed to turn up. In other words, *prejudice is a pre-condition of understanding* (278).

This conclusion is far-reaching as well as surprising, because Gadamer's framework, throughout the book, is a historical one. He is asking, not only how to interpret the words of others in general, but in particular, how to interpret texts that come down to us from the past. With respect to these, the suspension of prejudice takes the form of 'understanding historically' – that is, according to Gadamer, transposing oneself into the period when the statement was originally made so as to understand it as it will have been understood at the time. This too, he argues, is a withdrawal from dialogue:

> [T]he person understanding has, as it were, stopped trying to reach an agreement. He himself cannot be reached. By factoring the other person's standpoint into what he is claiming to say, we are making our own standpoint safely unattainable ... The text that is understood historically is forced to abandon its claim to be saying something true. We think we understand when we see the past from a historical standpoint – i.e., transpose ourselves into the historical situation and try to reconstruct the historical horizon. In fact, however, we have given up the claim to find in the past any truth that is valid and intelligible for ourselves. Acknowledging the otherness of the other in this way, making him the object of objective knowledge, involves the fundamental suspension of his claim to truth.
>
> (302–03)

Historicising the speech of the past, at least in the manner described here, removes it from any relation in which it might affect us as true (or, therefore, as false), and reduces it to a set of symptoms of the speaker's situation. This excludes the possibility that it might speak to *us*; the historical speaker is not our conversational partner but an object of our knowledge. Although it is only through his utterance that we know him, we render him mute. This suppression is a good example of the incompatibility between the two senses of 'understand': the (scientistic) understanding of objects and the (dialogic) understanding of speech. As Gadamer epigrammatically puts it later, 'When two people understand each other, this does not mean that one person "understands" the other.' (355) '"Understanding" the other' is a dominative relationship between consciousness and its object; 'understanding each other' is a mutual relationship between 'I' and 'thou' (352–55, 360–62).

But how does the second of these models apply to the understanding of writings from the past? The dialogue is surely metaphorical (though, as we shall see, Gadamer is not ultimately content to let it be *just* metaphorical). The text I read is fixed, my personal interlocutor is long dead and could not foresee me or my cultural references: in what sense might my encounter with the ancient words have the 'I – thou' character Gadamer's argument proposes? He offers at least one paradigm that makes the relationship easier to imagine: that of legal hermeneutics. Consider the position of a jurist reading an old law because of its bearing on a present case. Interpreting it does in a way involve 'historicising' it: if the text of the law uses a word in a sense that is now obsolete, for instance, or if some of its provisions are intelligible only in relation to other statutes that have since been repealed, then it is necessary to reconstruct its historical context so as not to misunderstand it. But the aim of such researches is definitely not to account for the text as an expression of the historical life that gave rise to it, or to restore the meanings that it had for its original readers. On the contrary, the jurist's purpose is precisely to establish what it means *now* – with what force it applies to the matter in hand.

Here then is a relationship between past text and present interpretation which can be meaningfully described as dialogic. The text is not 'understood' at the expense of its truth-claims: it is precisely because the interpreter regards it as a source of truth that he is at pains to interpret it as correctly as possible. The interpreter's standpoint is not kept safely out of the range of the text: rather, the point is that the text is authoritative, and the interpreter's standpoint is obliged to fall within the range of possibilities it permits. At the same time, though, the interpreter is very far from falling silent in the face of the text's authority. There is a new situation, a context of application presumably not envisaged by the original framers of the legislation, and this constitutes, in effect, the question that the interpreter is putting to the text. Nor is this question necessarily disinterested. The jurist may be in search of support for a particular line of argument; it is not as if he has no idea what he *wants* the statute to say, but he must find out, as it were, whether it is prepared to say it. The object of the hermeneutic exercise is, exactly, 'to reach an agreement', to arrive at a formula which does justice to the claims of both the old text and the new interest.

Legal interpretation thus furnishes Gadamer with a vividly suggestive model for the dialogic understanding of the words of the past. But it is also something of a special case, and it is worth pausing to note what its special conditions are. Most obviously, and as we saw in setting the case out, the text possesses authority; its interpreters cannot simply objectify it because *it* constrains *them*. They are professionally and as it were arbitrarily forced into dialogue with it. This compulsion is unusual. Gadamer's only other example of the same hermeneutic situation is a preacher's interpretation of Scripture: in that case too, evidently, there are particular reasons for regarding the text as authoritative.

These two instances, the jurist and the preacher, also share a second special condition: both kinds of interpretation take place within organisations that reproduce ancient texts as also current. So long as a statute or a judgment is still being invoked, it forms part of current legal discourse however long ago it was written; and a sacred text transcends historical difference more or less by definition. The dialogue of past text and present interpreter is readily possible, then, because the two share the same horizon, projected not out of contemporaneity but out of their belonging to the same temporally extended institution. Through the institution's longevity, time ceases to appear as what divides the present from the past, and operates instead as the connective medium through which things – objects, texts, meanings – are *handed down* to us. The ordinary term for the handing down is 'tradition'.

Although I have reached this concept via what I called the special case of legal hermeneutics, Gadamer makes it crucial to every kind of historical understanding. Tradition for him is the wavelength on which we converse with the voices of the past. It is because we belong to the same tradition as them that we do not merely overhear them talking to someone else, but hear them directly talking to us. It is because they belong to the same tradition as us that they are not alien objects we talk about, but interlocutors we address. We know what we can ask them. The resulting interaction, you could say, effectively *is* the tradition itself, the mechanism by which texts are handed down, and handed on. That is to say: for Gadamer, discourse as a whole is, or at any rate ought to be, characterised by the continuity which sustains an institution such as the law. His model of understanding as a dialogue is in that sense deeply conservative: it depends on social mechanisms whose very *raison d'être* is to conserve what comes down to us from the past.

TRADITION AND THE INDIVIDUAL TALENT

How might this conception of understanding inform the reading of literature in particular? Does Gadamer's model offer literature students a way of 'putting past and present into dialogue'? The special conditions of his juridical or religious analogy were, as we saw, that the old text possesses authority, and that some sort of historical institution assimilates it to a continuingly current discourse. Under what circumstances has the practice of literary understanding met these conditions?

One answer to that question can be found in T.S. Eliot's essay 'Tradition and the Individual Talent', which, for about half a century following its original appearance in 1919, exerted an immense influence on the way English literature was understood and taught. In part this influence was mediated by that of the critic and university teacher F.R. Leavis (1895–1978). Leavis could certainly not be described as Eliot's disciple, but his project did partly define itself in the terms Eliot had promulgated. His books included *Revaluation: Tradition and Development in English Poetry* (1936) and *The Great Tradition* (1948); both titles declared his adherence to Eliot's decisive concept. In turn, Leavis's students and followers produced the seven-volume *Pelican Guide to English Literature* (1954–61), which explicitly set out to 're-establish a sense of literary tradition' for a large non-specialist readership, and was much reprinted and revised throughout the 1960s and 1970s (Ford 1969: 7). Thus for almost a lifetime in the middle of the twentieth century, the idea of 'tradition' was essential to what English critics and teachers of literature thought they were doing.

Eliot's argument is that 'tradition and the individual talent' are intimately linked. No individual poet can be understood individually: 'his appreciation is the appreciation of his relation to the dead' (Eliot 1951: 15). A new poetic voice does not sound in empty space; it speaks, and is heard, in a room which is already populated by the words of its predecessors. Each significant writer becomes, as it were, a member of an already existing literary community; and this belonging is, paradoxically, both timeless (the poets of past centuries are all present for the newcomer) and intensely temporal (it is the *pastness* of these same poets that makes him especially conscious of his own contemporaneity). This community, extending through time and space, constantly assimilating difference but somehow always retaining its unity, is what Eliot means by 'tradition'. He maintains not only that an individual writer's work must conform to the tradition, but also, more surprisingly, that the tradition must conform to the individual writer's work:

> The existing monuments form an ideal order among themselves, which is modified by the introduction of the new (the really new) work of art among them. The existing order is complete before the new work arrives; for order to persist after the supervention of novelty, the *whole* existing order must be, if ever so slightly, altered; and so the relations, proportions, values of each work of art toward the whole are readjusted; and this is conformity between the old and the new. Whoever has approved this idea of order, of the form of European, of English literature will not find it preposterous that the past should be altered by the present as much as the present is directed by the past.

> (15)

Here, in English and literary terms, is a relationship with the texts of the past that closely resembles Gadamer's model. The new work of art fits in with the existing ones not despite its difference from them but precisely because of it: it draws them into fresh life by the conversation with them that it initiates. If a new work is not 'really' new, then it merely rehearses the meanings of the existing works, and there is no conversation because it is not, as it were, saying anything that they were not saying already. In short, what constitutes the 'conformity between the old and the new' is not compliance but dialogue.

Moreover, the conditions of possibility of this dialogue are the ones we have just derived from Gadamer's argument. The first is that the old texts 'handed down' to us possess authority. They are 'monuments', they constitute an 'order', they do not remain passively in the past but 'direct' the work of the present. A modern English poet, on this view, is not free *not* to read Donne, Milton, Wordsworth, and so on, because they are 'canonical': like the laws of a state or the sacred books of a religion, they form the necessary context of subsequent discourse. The second condition is that these authoritative texts are transmitted to the present and the future by a historically abiding institution, something like a court or a church, which makes the passage of centuries into a medium of connection rather than a measure of distance and difference. This is what is implied by Eliot's idea that 'the *whole* existing order' of literature reconfigures itself to accommodate each new arrival. The tradition is not simply a list of individual authors, but a quasi-organic whole made up of all the complex relations between them, a collective mind developing throughout the history of England or of Europe and always alive in the present: in short, it is *a literature*. Of course T.S. Eliot and John Donne are separated by an immense gap of time, of social and material circumstances, of ideology and language: the world of each, we could agree, is a 'foreign country' to the other. But in the passages of the great virtual edifice of literary tradition they can meet and come to an understanding. There, they are both at home.

At this point, though, the analogy gets strained. It requires 'English Literature' to form a transhistorical body, an institution analogous to a church or a college of law. In practice 'the tradition' has no such substance; its authority has no executive form; its power seems to come from its being imagined. Even Eliot and Leavis themselves, though they both sometimes speak about tradition as if they were describing something that simply exists, often seem rather to be envisaging something that does not. Their critical writings typically have a dissident edge: in different ways, both attack the culture of their own times for its disorder, or its rootlessness, or its modishness, as if the praise of tradition is addressed to readers who are in some way failing or refusing to recognise it. The date of Eliot's essay (1919) suggests the context of this emphasis: he was writing in the aftermath of the First World War, as we saw Hartley writing in the aftermath of the Second, and registering a comparable sense that the past had moved to the far side of an abyss. The 'handing down' is threatened by discontinuity and alienation; the reason it is being spoken about so vividly is precisely that it no longer goes without saying. The discourse of tradition, then, articulates need as much as accomplishment: where *is* the institution in which the cultural present can sustain its dialogue with the cultural past?

That question redirects us from the past that Eliot's essay contemplates to its own future reception. Over the following decades the study of English literature became at once more widespread and more culturally self-aware. In 1921, the Newbolt Report recommended that the teaching of English should be at the heart of the nation's newly compulsory secondary schools, and that literature should be at the heart of English. At a different level, the establishment of an English faculty at the University of Cambridge in 1926 marked the arrival of English literature as a fully recognised academic discipline (Baldick 1983: 92–108, 134–60). Leavis was contentiously involved in teaching at Cambridge from the mid-1920s onwards, and in 1943 he published *Education and the University: A Sketch for an 'English School'*, which offers detailed proposals for 'working out in practice at an ancient English university the means of rehabilitating the function of the "humanities"' (Leavis 1979: 19). It needs to be an 'ancient' university, he emphasises, because 'the preoccupation is not with the generalities of philosophical and moral theory and doctrine, but with picking up a continuity; carrying on and fostering the essential life of a time-honoured and powerful institution, in this concrete historical England.' Here Eliot's rather shadowy 'tradition' attains solid institutional form: as far as literature is concerned, the historical equivalent of the law courts and the church is to be the university.

Writing in 1943, Leavis was literally seeking to influence the post-war planning of higher education, and some of the subsequent developments did indeed reflect his argument. The university expansion of the 1960s made literature the dominant humanities degree subject. Typically, the syllabus combined the survey of a broad chronological range of English writing with a practice of unsystematically analytic reading; this combination was intended to give the student access to the national literature both as an object of general knowledge and as an immediate personal experience. In other words, the structure of the course was an expression of the relationship between tradition and the individual talent. Thus Eliot's essay, originally a quite sketchy periodical article, itself became a 'monument' of the kind it evokes, essential reading for the numerous inhabitants of the institution whose ideology it had prophetically articulated. The 'tradition', the space where the body of literature renews itself through dialogue with the individual and yet remains forever the same, was no longer a fanciful idealisation, but the rationale for a hundred English departments.

THE LIVES OF OTHERS

But once the departments came into existence, they placed the rationale under strain. To see how, it is worth staying a little longer with Leavis in wartime. He was thinking about the future of literary education as we have seen; he was also reading and responding to *Four Quartets*, Eliot's great poem about time and tradition, which appeared in stages in 1940–42; he was also, like everyone, asking, in conditions of heightened national self-consciousness, what cultural continuities could survive the conflagration that was taking place. Explaining the importance of the idea of tradition in a talk for social science students in 1943, he quoted the folklorist Cecil Sharp. During the First World War, Sharp had travelled in the American South and collected the songs that he published in *English Folk-Songs from the Southern Appalachians*. The people who sang them had, he says, long been 'shut off from all traffic with the rest of the world', and were largely illiterate, but also leisurely, sociable, graceful, eloquent, and deeply familiar with the Bible – in short, they were in Sharp's terms *cultured*. He goes on:

> The reason, I take it, why these mountain people, albeit unlettered, have acquired so many of the essentials of culture, is partly to be attributed to the large amount of leisure they enjoy, without which, of course, no cultural development is possible, but chiefly to the fact that they have one and all entered at birth into the full enjoyment of their racial inheritance. Their language, wisdom, manners and the many graces of life that are theirs, are merely racial attributes which have been gradually acquired and accumulated in past centuries and handed down generation by generation, each generation adding its quota to what it received ...
>
> ... Of the supreme value of an inherited tradition, even when unenforced by any formal school education, our mountain community in the Southern Highlands is an outstanding example.
>
> (Leavis 1952: 191)

An idyll is of course not a definition. These are the circumstances of a particular community, not the general requirements of tradition as such. But in citing them, Leavis gives them the force of a paradigm: this is what tradition at its finest could look and feel like. What is striking about the model he offers is that it is based on exceptional historical isolation. Geography, illiteracy, and Puritanism have combined to preserve the integrity of the transmission. There has been no foreign influence, no formal education, no printed book but the Bible, nothing to interrupt or complicate the accumulation of wisdom from one generation to the next. The generation that inherits, moreover, seems itself to be unanimous, untroubled by divisions about the interpretation or control of its inheritance – untroubled, that is to say, by politics. The singers Sharp meets in 1916 are unproblematically and directly the addressees of the eighteenth-century texts they perform; they are linguistically one with their mountain ancestors, far more than with their contemporaries in cities or on the Western Front. For them the past is not at all a foreign country: on the contrary, their native community extends easily through time in proportion to its confinement in space. This is especially dramatised by the fact that the artistic tradition in this case is an oral one: the appreciation of classic literature can be imagined as *literally* a dialogue, since it is a relationship between voice and voice, the interlocutors held together not only by verbal texts, but by tunes, vocal techniques, and proper occasions of performance. For the complex literary tradition Leavis is seeking to manage, mediated precisely by formal education and printed books, Sharp's account offers a sort of living metaphor.

But the institution that was to be host to the literary tradition was, so to speak, the very opposite of a mountain valley. As we have noted, English Literature did not form a closed community, but was expanding to the extent of becoming a mass subject in secondary and higher education. This was not simply a numerical matter: it also meant that students of literature and, later on, teachers of literature formed an increasingly diverse group in terms of their class, ethnicity, backgrounds, and attitudes. The community of inheritors, the collective to which tradition is handed down, was less and less a real entity. And if the sociological boundaries around English literature were becoming permeable, the cultural ones were no less so. As the student phenomenon of the 1960s made obvious, the internationalisation of the youth market and its associated media meant that universities were not sanctuaries from cultural 'traffic with the rest of the world', but just the opposite: global trading posts. Besides, one of the main motives prompting university expansion in general was the desire to become more socially mobile, and to that extent less rooted. In all these ways, higher education, including education in literature, was less a vessel for what is handed down to us than a means of breaking away from it. The effort to nominate the 'English School' as the institutional medium of literary tradition was always against this grain.

As is very well known, the discipline's response to this unsustainable contradiction was what is largely and vaguely referred to as 'theory'. That is, during the 1970s and 1980s, the 'traditional' modes and aims of literary teaching and criticism were challenged, and often overthrown, by an irregular but remarkably powerful revaluation that drew its critical concepts, not from the English literary past, but from the European intellectual makers of modernity and postmodernity: Nietzsche, Marx, Freud, Foucault, Derrida. This movement was fertile in self-description, so there is neither space nor need to attempt a general account of it here (Eagleton 1996 [1983]; Lodge and Wood 2008 [1988]). But one aspect of it is of immediate interest to us: its redefinition of the academy's relationship with the literature of the past.

What happened was that the concept of tradition, dominant as we have seen for a long mid-century generation, rapidly lost its power to order and illuminate. To put the matter confrontationally: an ordinary undergraduate seminar, presented today with Leavis's quotation from Sharp, would have immediate political objections to its language. The vision of 'handing down', after all, implies an enduring principle of connection between those who bequeath the value and those who inherit it; and the connection that the metaphor most naturally suggests is a genetic one. Tradition casts the writers of the past as *our* ancestors, and *us* as their descendants. Together, across the centuries, we constitute a collective unity of some kind, and how are we to imagine that? As a nation, a people, a race? Literary theory and liberal politics concur in questioning this dubious transhistorical essence. Whom, for instance, does it exclude? Perhaps understandably, then, current mainstream guides to critical vocabulary, such as the series to which this book is a contribution, tend not to include the word 'tradition' in their lists. Its replacement, as the indispensable term in the understanding of the literary past, is 'culture'.

This is a concept that has itself experienced many vicissitudes and revaluations over the last fifty years or so. But an arrival of a fairly decisive kind was marked when the influential University of Chicago Press *Critical Terms for Literary Study* began its second edition (1996) with the formal announcement that a long predicted 'cultural turn' in literary studies had occurred. Literature was now to be regarded, not as an autonomous art form, but as one cultural practice among others. The implications of this 'turn' are suggested by the article on 'Culture' in the same volume. It is by the leading exponent of 'cultural poetics', Stephen Greenblatt, who appears in much of his work as a various, interrogative and interestingly discontented critic; here, however, the generalising brief and the limited space combine to incline him to the schematic. He proposes a set of 'cultural questions' that might be asked about a work from the past:

> What kinds of behavior, what models of practice, does this work seem to enforce?
>
> Why might readers at a particular time and place find this work compelling?
>
> Are there differences between my values and the values implicit in the work I am reading?
>
> Upon what social understandings does the work depend?
>
> Whose freedom of thought or movement might be constrained implicitly or explicitly by this work?
>
> What are the larger social structures with which these particular acts of praise or blame might be connected?
>
> (Lentricchia and McLaughlin 1995: 226)

The last of these questions is in a sense the destination of the others: after setting out the list, Greenblatt adds, 'Eventually, a full cultural analysis will need to push beyond the boundaries of the text, to establish links between the text and values, institutions and practices elsewhere in the culture.' Joining up 'particular acts' and 'larger structures' is the project to which the subordinate questions are designed to contribute.

Clearly the work of art belongs to 'the culture'. In a recurrent spatial metaphor, it is situated *within* it, and the contained work and the containing culture have the capacity to shed light on one another: 'If an exploration of a particular culture will lead to a heightened understanding of a work of literature produced within that culture, so too a careful reading of a work of literature will lead to a heightened understanding of the culture within which it was produced.' (227) But it is equally clear that the student-reader of the work does *not* belong to 'the culture'; he or she is assumed to be outside it, investigating it, establishing its internal links and unearthing its implicit laws. All Greenblatt's questions are about the work's relationship, not with the reader who is invited to ask them, but with the inhabitants of the culture within which the work was produced. *They* are the readers it compels or constrains or defers to. We, the students of literature in pursuit of 'cultural understanding', are for that very reason not the ones the work of literature addresses. Rather, we are *eavesdropping*.

This, you could say, is the outsider's hermeneutics: the reader is not the inheritor of a warmly indigenous tradition, but the product of an ordinarily divided modern society, whose experience is that the monuments of English literature seem on the whole to be talking to somebody else. That is indeed the way this distancing identification of 'a' culture is often used in practice. Greenblatt himself is, sometimes explicitly, a Jewish reader of predominantly Christian culture, but the same coolly external standpoint may serve a working-class reader of predominantly patrician culture, a colonised reader of predominantly imperial culture, or (to cite the situation of a sizeable majority of British literature students) a woman reading a culture dominated by men. And so it goes on: black reading white; gay reading straight; Celtic reading English. Eventually it appears that there are no insiders left: that all reading is 'cultural' reading in this estranged and estranging sense.

Two further features of Greenblatt's exposition, also representative of 'the cultural turn', deepen this gulf between the student and the text. The first is the evident hostility with which the questions are framed. The work, it is assumed, 'enforces' certain kinds of behaviour and 'constrains' some people's freedom of thought or movement. Understanding it, then, means understanding what tasks of control and containment it is performing on behalf of its culture, in other words, how it is working to diminish human freedom. Criticism is therefore a kind of resistance, and this recalls my earlier shortlist of modern fathers of 'theory'. Nietzsche, Marx, Freud, Foucault, and Derrida form an eclectic pantheon in many ways, but one thing they have in common is that they all offer conceptual frameworks for what has been called the hermeneutics of suspicion: the practice of interpreting utterances not so as to restore the meanings the words were intended to express, but so as to uncover the meanings the words were designed to conceal. For all of them, the most urgently interesting thing about a text is not what it deliberately conveys but what it inadvertently betrays. There is no question, here, of partners in a dialogue 'coming to an understanding'. Rather, the critic is a covert listener, intercepting messages meant for others' ears, cracking the enemy's codes.

Second, the reader's estrangement from the literary text is confirmed by the implication, which I think is not theoretically necessary but is insistent in practice, that the concept of 'a culture' is a synchronic one. When Greenblatt speaks of values and practices 'elsewhere in the culture', he means values and practices that can be retrieved from other documents and artefacts of the same *time*. When he hopes that growing interdisciplinarity will make it more possible 'for students to reach toward a sense of the complex whole of a particular culture' (230), he is conceiving of a miscellany of actions as constituting a 'whole' and 'particular' object of understanding because of the chronological boundaries that confine them all together: the undeclared principle of unity of a culture is simultaneity. Consequently the idea of a tradition, that is, a *diachronic* cultural totality, is methodologically excluded: it is literally inexpressible in the terms Greenblatt is proposing. If a culture is a chronologically defined state of affairs, then it is impossible for me to share in Shakespeare's culture just as it is impossible for me to go back to last Thursday. The past is a foreign country absolutely and by definition.

Like the practice of 'suspicious' reading, this operating assumption follows intelligibly from some of the intellectual sources of the 'cultural turn'. 'New historicism' in particular adopted anthropology as a sort of mentor discipline for understanding the literature of the past: the Renaissance could be imagined as a temporal Pacific island whose social practices and artistic conventions became intelligible as the investigator made out their symbolic functions in the life of the community. It is an enlivening analogy, but it casts the critic as the studious visitor, observing everything with notebook in hand: however industriously the observer participates, the tribal oratory is not really addressed to *him*. Archaeology offered another model, partly because of its prominence as a metaphor in the methodological writings of Michel Foucault. It too has the effect of constructing historical periods as discrete entities, layers filled with objects that are meaningful only as fragments of the past culture that can be deduced from them. To 'read' a recovered object is not to enter into any direct relationship with it, but to infer its relationships with other objects found at the same depth. Unless we can fix their meaning at their own level, they remain mute.

Disappointingly but unsurprisingly, then, the widespread effect of unpicking the idea of tradition is to silence the dialogue of past and present. For Gadamer, understanding in the humanities meant not the dominative knowledge of the properties of an object, but the effort to come to an agreement with other speakers by engaging in dialogue with them through the medium of tradition. If tradition cannot serve as such a medium, then the dialogue is blocked, and the understanding of the past reverts to the scientific model whose hegemony Gadamer was seeking to outflank. The verbal life of the past is reduced to a silent object of our masterly present knowing.

GETTING INTO CONVERSATION

It seems, then, that as the idea of a literary tradition loses its persuasiveness, it leaves the study of literature in a blind alley. Without a tradition – that is, without an enduring institution that brings texts and readers together across historical time – the dialogue of present and past falls silent. As readers in that silence, we either acknowledge the otherness of the past and therefore, as Gadamer put it, 'give up the claim to find in the past any truth that is valid and intelligible for ourselves' (303); or else, frustrated by that alienation, we *refuse* to acknowledge the otherness of the past, and insist on treating its literary traces as if they expressed and addressed a world exactly like our own. In the first case, the past doesn't speak to us, and in the second case, what speaks to us is not the past.

The educational implications of this dilemma are serious enough to question the central place of literature in the humanities curriculum. In its simplest form, the question is whether the writings of the past are capable of meaning anything to present readers. On the first horn of the dilemma – the insistence on the otherness of other times – students learn that it is impossible to understand old poems and stories without a cultural historian on hand to explain what they once meant. Commentary talks over the voices of the past; the lesson is that in themselves they are inaudible. On the second horn – the *refusal* of the otherness of other times – students learn to realise the meaning of an old poem or story by detaching it from its history and attaching it to their own. This is sometimes called 'relevance'; the lesson is that we can understand the writings of the past only to the extent that they cease to be of the past. As often happens with binary oppositions of this kind, the more you look at these alternatives, the less different they appear. The capacity of past and present to talk to each other is blocked off either way. The trouble with that is not only that the writings of the Renaissance, or the Victorians, get sealed into their respective airtight 'cultures'. It is also, more damagingly, that we become trapped in our own. To get out of this cul-de-sac, I suggest in conclusion that we return to Bakhtin.

There is a moment in 'Discourse in the Novel' when he is pursuing the idea that no individual speaker ever encounters 'a single unitary language, inviolable and indisputable' (*DI* 295). Rather, the universal heteroglot environment means that everyone faces 'the necessity of *having to choose a language*.' One's words are never just given. To make this thought clearer, he imagines what the contrary would be like:

> Only by remaining in a closed environment, one without writing or thought, completely off the maps of socio-ideological becoming, could a man fail to sense this activity of selecting a language and rest assured in the inviolability of his own language, the conviction that his language is predetermined.

A really unitary language presupposes conditions of absolute seclusion, a speech community somehow untouched by history. Even in such a community, though, Bakhtin adds with characteristic obstinacy, there would really be several languages, not just one:

> Thus an illiterate peasant, miles away from any urban center, naively immersed in an unmoving and for him unshakable everyday world, nevertheless lived in several language systems: he prayed to God in one language (Church Slavonic), sang songs in another, spoke to his family in a third and, when he began to dictate petitions to the local authorities through a scribe, he tried speaking yet a fourth language (the official-literate language, 'proper' language). All these are *different languages*, even from the point of view of abstract socio-dialectological markers. But these languages were not dialogically coordinated in the linguistic consciousness of the peasant; he passed from one to the other without thinking, automatically: each was indisputably in its own place, and the place of each was indisputable. He was not yet able to regard one language (and the verbal world corresponding to it) through the eyes of another language.
>
> (*DI* 295–96)

This Russian backwater, explicitly a hypothetical extreme, is recognisably the same kind of place as Leavis's Southern Appalachian valley. Both exist behind closed cultural borders, where the absence of literacy and urbanisation means that textual transmission takes the form of songs and devotions. And in both cases the effect of the closure is a sort of homeostasis, a 'verbal world' that never experiences lack, or excess, or novelty, but is always self-complete. But the parallel locations embody opposing values. Whereas Leavis's enclave contains, as we have seen, a special richness of tradition, Bakhtin's exemplifies a special linguistic poverty. On the one hand, it is just because the Appalachian community is cut off from historical becoming that it enjoys its easy commerce of the old and the new; it understands and performs and augments its inherited stock in conditions of uninterrupted continuity; its interpretation of the ancient songs denies neither their antiquity nor their truth, but meets with them in an equal dialogue. On the other hand, that same separation from history deprives the Russian peasant of any linguistic consciousness at all, condemning him to an endless discursive present, where nothing that is said could imaginably be said differently. His various languages co-exist in 'a state of peaceful and moribund equilibrium' because each one is inescapably determined by its context of utterance. Consequently, he never 'regards one language through the eyes of another language'; his speech world is devoid of dialogue. Thus where Leavis and Sharp see the conditions of a precious continuity, Bakhtin sees a primordial desert where the real life of language has not yet begun.

In these ironically diverging utopias, we can see the sharply different emphases that are latent in the idea of dialogue. When Gadamer invokes it as the means of understanding the written utterances of the past, he is emphasising community. To develop a dialogue, the interlocutors need at least the elements of a common language, a shared understanding of what the conversation is about and what counts as a valid contribution to it, and a shared intention (though it may be frustrated) of reaching agreement. Without these conditions, you don't have dialogue, but some other kind of verbal interaction: reciprocal interruption, say, or the objectifying description of one speaker by another. It is natural enough, then, that Gadamer's account of historical understanding as dialogue across time depends on the concept of tradition: that is what sustains the requisite shared understandings between interlocutors in different ages. Without tradition, no common language; without a common language, no dialogue. It is by virtue of what we share with our forebears that we are able to get into conversation with them.

For Bakhtin, on the other hand, dialogue is above all a mark of the linguistic diversity that both informs and confronts the act of speaking; in invoking it, he characteristically emphasises disjunction. To develop a dialogue, the interlocutors need to be genuinely *outside* one another; their respective languages must be distinct, and articulate distinct verbal-ideological worlds. Without these conditions, you don't have dialogue, but a merely formal imitation of it (*DI* 327). Naturally enough, then, Bakhtin's literary history turns typically not so much on the idea of tradition as on that of hybridisation. For him, literary forms typically arise, or mutate, or realise their potential, when languages bump into each other: ecclesiastical and commercial, official and colloquial, Greek and Latin, poetic and journalistic. These encounters are the linguistic dimension of historical change: the migration of peoples, the effects of trade, the tension-filled mutual awareness of social groups, and so on. Without disruption, no heteroglossia; without heteroglossia, no dialogue.

This opposition is a matter of emphasis, not of flat disagreement. Gadamer is not denying that the participants in a dialogue are necessarily different from one another, and Bakhtin is not denying that they are necessarily comprehensible to one another. But the change in emphasis is nevertheless decisive. For in Bakhtin's model the dialogues that really matter happen not within a tradition, not at the heart of a cultural continuity secured from outside interference by institutional walls or mountain passes, but precisely at the point of outside interference. It is in the process of distinguishing itself from what it is not that a 'tradition' defines itself. 'Traffic with the rest of the world' doesn't dissipate or contaminate it; on the contrary, it *constitutes* it. In another Bakhtinian epigram, 'The realm of culture has no internal territory; it is entirely distributed along the boundaries' (Emerson 1997: 301). If that is so, it follows that we will find the literary text in its full significance and seriousness, neither in the foreign country of 'its own' culture nor in the deep home of 'our own' tradition, but at a border crossing, where several dialects compete for acceptance and no sovereignty is comprehensive.

What does that mean in practice? Most simply, it means thinking of both our opposed concepts, 'tradition' and 'culture', in the plural. Take 'tradition' first. I mentioned that the idea, traceable to Eliot's essay, of an organically coherent literary tradition, spanning the centuries and dictating the curriculum, lost its power to order and illuminate during the political and theoretical upheavals that characterised literary studies in the 1970s and 1980s. But I could have added that in the same period the concept of a sectional or dissident 'tradition' was *plurally* very active. For example, there were pioneering surveys or anthologies of writing by women, or from the differing communities of Ireland, or of societies where English is the literary language because it was imposed by colonialism (e.g., Gilbert and Gubar 1979; Spender and Todd 1989; Field Day 1991–2002; Thieme 1996).

Or again, there were studies that tried to unearth, within or behind the official canon of literature and drama, popular traditions of narrative and entertainment, or secretive traditions of dissident sexuality (e.g., Bradby *et al.* 1980; Bristol 1989; Sedgwick 1985; Woods 1998). All these enterprises were informed by a desire to claim certain writers of the past as forebears, so this was tradition in very much the sense we recognise from Gadamer: a trans-historical shared horizon in virtue of which writer and reader address one another directly, the communally handed-down medium of a conversation with the honoured dead. But the difference was that these 'traditions' are, like Bakhtin's languages, neither pre-determined nor unitary: they are chosen, and they define them-selves, in relation to more powerful antithetic traditions – male, British, imperial, elite, straight. The relation may be militant, or collusive, or dutiful, or parodic, but in any event it is inescapable. In short, tradition in this context is *dialogic*.

If 'the' tradition we saw in Eliot is thus pluralised, so equally is 'the' culture, the unitary synchronic object that we saw in Greenblatt. Cultural dialogue for Bakhtin is acted out over great tracts of time: a proposition can wait centuries for the rejoinder that will animate its meaning. Homer was memorised and quoted in Plato's Athens; classical Latin interacted with the European vernaculars of the Renaissance; the nineteenth-century Russian novel crossed the ancient rhythms of oral story-telling with the French accents of upper-class enlightenment. No age is simply contemporary with itself; historical time is not really organised in horizontal layers like an office-block; every present is full of its own past, and reaches out towards its future. It follows that when a significant work of literature first appears, it is not yet complete. Bakhtin thinks of a literary masterpiece as a slow-release device, whose semantic potential is realised bit by bit as successive interlocutors engage it in different kinds of dialogue. For example, *Don Quixote*, as we saw in an earlier chapter, is a kind of founda-tional myth for the novel as a genre: its ironic management of the relationship between writing and action has turned out to be paradigmatic. But of course it had no such significance when it was first published, because at that point there was no novel genre for it to be in that relationship with. It came to have these meanings much later, when it was *answered* in a way that understood them. Thus a historicism that confines the work to 'its own' synchronically conceived culture cuts short the meeting with others that elicits its full seriousness and vitality: as Bakhtin put it in a late essay, 'Everything that belongs only to the present dies along with the present.' (Bakhtin 1986: 4)

'Tradition' and 'culture', in short, are not monolithic entities which either include us or stand over against us: they are both, themselves, unevenly developing conversations that are already going on. Understanding them, then, is a matter neither of deferring to them (only the past speaks) nor of knowing them as objects (only the present speaks), but rather of getting into the conversation (past and present speak to each other). This is to imagine that getting to know a book is something like getting to know a person: it is done not by silently observing the other, but by engaging him, or her, in co-operation, argument, question-and-answer, a process which entails showing a good deal of oneself at the same time.

In some ways, this principle is necessarily a metaphorical one (on the whole, people don't actually have conversations with books). But the academy provides at least one respect in which it is flatly literal: the literary essay. Almost by formal definition, this genre, the only one that students of literature routinely practise themselves, contains two alternating voices: that of the text that is being quoted or paraphrased, and that of the student-critic who is interpreting it. The alternation is in Bakhtinian terms unfinalised. On the one hand, as a critic, coming on the scene later, I can judge the literary text as it cannot judge me. But on the other hand the text, being the true subject of my essay, is as it were inherently evidential: if I describe it wrongly, it exposes my error simply by being what it is. The two discourses exercise *different kinds* of authority, and for that reason their interaction has the to-and-fro character of dialogue. At this point, the dialogic forms of writing I discussed much earlier in this book reappear as it were directly under our hands. Like a novelist orchestrating authorial and characteral intonations, or like a composer of Socratic dialogue assigning different points of view to different blocks of text on the page, the critic needs to move between positions inside and outside the book under consideration.

This even extends to a measure of internal dialogisation. For example, if you look back at the opening of this book, you will see that the third paragraph ends with this sentence about the Comte de Mirabeau: 'He was the man of the moment because he had talked himself into it.' Who says so? Although I wrote the sentence, it is not my judgment of Mirabeau, but my exposition of Kleist's judgment of Mirabeau. So the answer is that it is Kleist who says so. But on the other hand, the play on the phrase 'to talk oneself into something' is not Kleist's; it is both English and modern, and it has no detailed counterpart in Kleist's essay. So in saying what Kleist said I am also speaking myself, bringing out, in my own words, what Kleist's words seem to me to assume or imply. That is, the sentence is a mixture of my voice and Kleist's. It is a mixture, moreover, whose exact proportions are uncertain. The reader may guess that I share Kleist's view, but I have not said so: it is also possible that I am expounding it in order to attack it, or that I do not intend to express my own view at all. Most people who write literary essays, whether as students or as published critics, are used to managing this kind of ambiguity. Paraphrasing, glossing, extrapolating, are ordinary functions of my practice as a critic, and they easily produce moments when it is not quite clear whether I am speaking 'as myself' or as the author I am interpreting. The doubt is the product of an interplay between the critic's word and the author's which is structurally very similar to the interplay between the author's word and the character's within a fictional text. In that sense, a critic writes like a novelist.

In other words, dialogic form is not only something that as students of literature we constantly come across; it is also something that we do. It is the form *of* the critical writer's uneasy position on the boundaries between cultures, between traditions. This is not to say that dialogue is the means of resolving the contradictions we have been exploring. It is something more helpful than that: a way of living humanely and coherently with their not being resolved.

Glossary

Some help with the specialist vocabulary of this book may be useful. On the other hand, anyone who accepts the main lines of its argument is likely to approach glossaries with mistrust. Words mean things in the interactions of speakers; definition, with its air of brisk finality, abstracts them from the life of language and accords them a misleading fixity. To counteract this effect, I have where possible referred readers to a more open-ended treatment of the word in the body of the text.

dialogism The principle, elaborated above all by Bakhtin, that speech is formed not by a single speaker but by the interaction of multiple speakers with differing intentions and meanings. Any text that exemplifies this principle can be described as **dialogic**. When the word of one speaker is relativised or divided by interference from the word of another, it is **dialogised**. See pp. 48–50.

direct speech 'Direct' and 'indirect' denote opposed ways of representing another person's speech. **Direct speech** asks to be taken as the original speaker's exact words. **Indirect speech** claims to report the substance of what the original speaker said, but the exact words are those of the reporter. Indirect speech is therefore latently double-voiced in a way that direct speech is not: in it, the reported voice and the reporting voice are heard together. See pp. 39–42.

discourse In many contexts, 'discourse' means language *considered as someone's activity*: it is called 'language' when it is viewed as an abstract system, but 'discourse' when the words and grammatical rules are caught up in the actual business of saying something. The word is also often used to refer to a socially or functionally distinctive set of verbal conventions: thus, the 'discourses' of prayer, gossip and scientific enquiry are all different, even if all these communicative activities are being carried on in the same language.

double-voicing A Bakhtinian term for what is happening when, within a text, two distinct speakers can be identified as the source of the same utterance. The most straightforward kind of double-voicing, though by no means the only kind, is parody.

Enlightenment The decisive intellectual and cultural movement of the eighteenth century in Europe, centrally in France. It criticised customary or arbitrary faith from the standpoint of reason and direct experience, and was later criticised in its turn for its faith in the knowability of the world. See pp. 24–6.

epic Narrative, as opposed to dramatic, poetry. The paradigmatic classical examples are Homer and Virgil, so the term also implies that the narrative is about semi-legendary heroes. See pp. 57–8.

epic theatre Bertolt Brecht's name for his new way of writing and performing plays, since it was designed to help the theatre acquire the artistic advantages of narrative form. See pp. 117–21.

heteroglossia A Bakhtinian coinage denoting the dynamic multiplicity of language in use. See p. 50.

ideology A system of ideas and values, and, in particular, such a system considered as *socially effective* – that is, as serving the interests of a particular social group, and as articulated in such a way as to prevail over other, conflicting, systems of ideas and values.

illocution J.L. Austin's term for an utterance insofar as it constitutes an action, such as warning, ordering. or adjudicating. The capacity of the utterance to work as an action is its *illocutionary force*. See p. 94.

indirect speech see **direct speech**

interlocutor Interlocutors are the persons engaged in a dialogue. My interlocutor is the person I am talking to, or with.

lyric Strictly, poetry that is designed to be sung; but within the classical genre system the word serves to identify almost any poetry which, being neither narrative nor dramatic, can be understood as expressing the mind of its author directly.

modernity 'Modern' is a *differential* marker of time: it means 'now' as opposed to 'then', and depending on the context, the dividing line between the two may be world war, industrialisation, Enlightenment, or even the fall of classical Rome. The concept of 'modernity' generalises the opposition: it refers to the experience of historical newness, the sense that things will never be the same again.

monologic Having the form of a monologue, single-voiced. And in Bakhtinian terms, resistant to dialogism. 'Monologic' texts, speakers and institutions are those that assume, or try to impose, a direct and uncontested relationship between words and meanings. See pp. 52–6.

object Grammatically speaking, any transitive verb has a subject and an object. If the verb itself represents a 'doing', the subject names the entity that does it, and the object specifies the entity to which it is done. By extension, 'subject' and 'object' in many kinds of philosophic discourse denote the active and passive parties to a transaction such as sensory perception, desire, representation, or knowledge. Thus the 'subject' of knowledge is the one who knows, and the 'object' of knowledge is whatever it is that is known. To confine another's being to the object position in such a transaction is to **objectify** the other.

parody A discourse that mocks another discourse by imitating it, and therefore contains two voices at once, that of the one who is parodied and that of the parodist. See pp. 101–2.

performative An utterance which is performing an action rather than stating a proposition, and must therefore be judged effectual or ineffectual rather than true or false. See pp. 93–4.

rhetoric The formal study and practice of effective speech, as it was taught in classical Greece and Rome, and in medieval and Renaissance Europe. By extension, the word can apply, sometimes but not always with derogatory overtones, to any instance of language being used pragmatically or persuasively rather than with regard to referential accuracy. See pp. 21–3.

subject see **object**

tradition The process by which works of art, texts, meanings, or beliefs are handed down and reconfigured from one generation to the next, thus sustaining a community over time. See pp. 133–5.

utterance The general term to cover anything that is said by someone, regardless of whether it is spoken or written.

FURTHER READING

MIKHAIL BAKHTIN, *THE DIALOGIC IMAGINATION*

A collection of four essays on the aesthetics of the novel. Bakhtin wrote them between 1934 and 1941, and they were published in Russian in 1975 under the title *Questions of Literature and Aesthetics*; the English title was supplied by the translators. For our purposes, the most important of the four is the earliest and longest, 'Discourse in the Novel', which is Bakhtin's most extended and systematic statement of the theory that the novel is both inherently and historically a dialogic form.

MIKHAIL BAKHTIN, *PROBLEMS OF DOSTOEVSKY'S POETICS*

Dostoevsky is for Bakhtin the dialogic novelist *par excellence*, so this book shows what the idea means in practice, as well as offering a dazzling genealogy of Dostoevskian narrative going back to classical times. The book was first published in 1929, but Bakhtin revised it for a new edition in 1963, which is the basis of the English translation. Consequently, this version includes clarifying responses to some of the original reviews, and also, as an appendix, some compressed but far-reaching notes that Bakhtin made while working on the revision in 1961.

DEBORAH CAMERON, *GOOD TO TALK? LIVING AND WORKING IN A COMMUNICATION CULTURE*

This sociolinguistic study is about talk rather than dialogue strictly defined. Published at the zenith of New Labour, it takes on the cultural and managerial orthodoxies that represent all social problems as problems of communication and promote informal, sincere conversation as a general panacea. Cameron's critique is hard-hitting and very funny.

VIRGINIA COX, *THE RENAISSANCE DIALOGUE: LITERARY DIALOGUE IN ITS SOCIAL AND POLITICAL CONTEXTS, CASTIGLIONE TO GALILEO*

A scholarly account, at once encyclopedically informative and conceptually alert, of dialogue as a literary form in sixteenth- and seventeenth-century Italy.

DENIS DIDEROT, *THE PARADOX OF THE ACTOR* AND *RAMEAU'S NEPHEW*

I have not managed to find space to discuss these dialogues, but they are especially fine examples of what the genre can be made to do. Coming out of the intensely conversational culture of Enlightenment Paris, they dramatise the pleasures of intellectual improvisation.

HANS-GEORG GADAMER, *TRUTH AND METHOD*

This book investigates a simple but profound question: what does it mean to understand something? It is a monumental work, so deeply engaged with its German philosophical tradition as to be hard going for the non-specialist. But as well as integrating the idea of dialogue in an immense system, it is also capable of startling, epigrammatic conciseness.

VIMALA HERMAN, *DRAMATIC DISCOURSE: DIALOGUE AS INTERACTION IN PLAYS*

A theoretically sophisticated application of linguistic terminology to the scripts of a wide range of modern drama.

MICHAEL MACOVSKI (ED.), *DIALOGUE AND CRITICAL DISCOURSE: LANGUAGE, CULTURE, CRITICAL THEORY*

A wide-ranging collection of essays, mostly literary in focus, on the theoretical implications of the idea of dialogue.

JÜRGEN MITTELSTRASS, 'ON SOCRATIC DIALOGUE', IN CHARLES L. GRISWOLD (ED.), *PLATONIC WRITINGS – PLATONIC READINGS*

This brief essay gives a clear and provocative explanation of the *philosophical* reasons for writing philosophy in dialogue form.

W.J. ONG, *ORALITY AND LITERACY*

What are the important differences, semantically and culturally, between the spoken and the written forms of the word? This book is the indispensable introduction to that question.

PETER SZONDI, *THEORY OF THE MODERN DRAMA*

This short, classic book lucidly traces the formation and subsequent break-up of the European dramatic convention characterised by 'the absolute dominance of dialogue'.

TZVETAN TODOROV, *MIKHAIL BAKHTIN: THE DIALOGICAL PRINCIPLE*

On the whole, the best way to grasp Bakhtin's ideas is to read Bakhtin himself; but this book is the exception. Todorov actively reads, translates, and reorganises Bakhtin while still allowing his voice to come through with extraordinary accuracy.

ROWAN WILLIAMS, *WHY STUDY THE PAST?*

A series of lectures by the Archbishop of Canterbury, exploring the Church's relationship with its past, and the difficult mixture of permanence and discontinuity that constitutes its historical identity. Some of the issues discussed in my final chapter are developed here in a different context with both subtlety and authority.

Bibliography

Archer, William, 1926. *Play-Making: A Manual of Craftsmanship*, 3rd edition [1st edition 1912]. London: Chapman and Hall.

Aristotle, 1965. *On the Art of Poetry*, in *Classical Literary Criticism*, tr. and ed. T.S. Dorsch. Penguin.

Austin, J.L., 1975. *How to Do Things with Words*, 2nd edition [1st edition 1962]. Oxford: Oxford University Press.

Bakhtin, Mikhail, 1981. *The Dialogic Imagination*, ed. Michael Holquist, tr. Caryl Emerson and Michael Holquist. Austin: University of Texas Press.

——, 1984. *Problems of Dostoevsky's Poetics*, ed. and tr. Caryl Emerson. Manchester: Manchester University Press.

——, 1986. *Speech Genres and Other Late Essays*, tr. Vern W. McGee. Austin: University of Texas Press.

Baldick, Chris, 1983. *The Social Mission of English Criticism 1848–1932*. Oxford: Clarendon Press.

Bohm, David, 2004. *On Dialogue*. Routledge Classics edition. London: Routledge.

Bradby, David, James, Louis and Sharratt, Bernard, 1980. *Performance and Politics in Popular Drama: Aspects of Popular Entertainment in Theatre, Film, and Television, 1800–1976*. Cambridge: Cambridge University Press.

Brandist, Craig, 2002. *The Bakhtin Circle: Philosophy, Culture, Politics*. London: Pluto Press.

Brecht, Bertolt, 1962. *Mother Courage and her Children*, translated by Eric Bentley. London: Methuen.

——, 1964. *Brecht on Theatre: the Development of an Aesthetic*, edited and translated by John Willett. London: Methuen.

——, 1967. *Gesammelte Werke*, Band 9. Frankfurt am Main: Suhrkamp.

Bristol, Michael D., 1989. *Carnival and Theater: Plebeian Culture and the Structure of Authority in Renaissance England*. London: Routledge.

Burke, Peter, 1995. *The Fortunes of the Courtier: the European Reception of Castiglione's Cortegiano*. London: Polity Press.

Cameron, Deborah, 2000. *Good to Talk? Living and Working in a Communication Culture*. London: Sage Publications.

Carroll, Lewis, 1998. *Alice's Adventures in Wonderland and Through the Looking-Glass*. London: Penguin.

Castiglione, Baldesar, 1967. *The Book of the Courtier*, tr. George Bull. London: Penguin.

Cervantes, Miguel de, 1998. *The History and Adventures of the Renowned Don Quixote*, tr. Tobias Smollett. Ware: Wordsworth Editions.

Chekhov, Anton, 1983. *Three Sisters*, tr. Michael Frayn. London: Methuen.

Cicero, Marcus Tullius, 1942. *De Oratore*, 2 vols, tr. E.W. Sutton and H. Rackham, Loeb Classical Library. Cambridge, MA: Harvard University Press.

Cook, Michael, 2000. *The Koran: A Very Short Introduction*. Oxford: Oxford University Press.

Cox, Virginia, 1992. *The Renaissance Dialogue: Literary Dialogue in its Social and Political Contexts, Castiglione to Galileo*. Cambridge: Cambridge University Press.

Craig, Edward Gordon, 1962. *On the Art of the Theatre*. London: Mercury Books.

Dentith, Simon, 1995. *Bakhtinian Thought: an Introductory Reader*. London: Routledge.

Dickens, Charles, 1948. *Bleak House*. Oxford: Oxford University Press.

Diderot, Denis, 1966. *Rameau's Nephew and D'Alembert's Dream*, tr. Leonard Tancock. London: Penguin.

——, 1994. *The Paradox of the Actor*, in *Selected Writings on Art and Literature*, tr. Geoffrey Bremner. London: Penguin.

Eagleton, Terry, 1996. *Literary Theory: An Introduction*, revised edn [1st edition 1983]. Oxford: Blackwell.

Elam, Keir, 1980. *The Semiotics of Theatre and Drama*. London: Methuen.

Eliot, T.S., 1951. *Selected Essays*, 3rd edn. London: Faber and Faber.

Emerson, Caryl, 1997. *The First Hundred Years of Mikhail Bakhtin*. Princeton, NJ: Princeton University Press.

Farquhar, George, 1995. *The Constant Couple*, in *The Recruiting Officer and Other Plays*, ed. William Myers. Oxford: Oxford University Press.

Field Day, 1991–2002. *The Field Day Anthology of Irish Writing*, general editor Seamus Deane; associate editors Andrew Carpenter, Jonathan Williams. 5 vols. London: Faber.

Fielding, Henry, 1999. *Joseph Andrews and Shamela*. London: Penguin.

——, 1966. *Tom Jones*. London: Penguin.

Fielding, K.J. and Brice, Alec W., 1968–69. 'Charles Dickens on "The Exclusion of Evidence"', *The Dickensian*, 64 (1968), 131–40 and 65 (1969), 35–41.

Finocchiaro, Maurice A., 1989. *The Galileo Affair: A Documentary History*. Berkeley: University of California Press.

Ford, Boris (ed.), 1969. *The Pelican Guide to English Literature 6: From Dickens to Hardy*, reprint with revisions. London: Penguin.

Fuentes, Carlos, 1989. 'Words apart', *Guardian*, 24 February.

Gadamer, Hans-Georg, 2004. *Truth and Method*, tr. Joel Weinsheimer and Donald G. Marshall [translation first published 1989]. London and New York: Continuum.

Galilei, Galileo, 1962. *Dialogue concerning the Two Chief World Systems – Ptolemaic and Copernican*, tr. Stillman Drake. Berkeley: University of California Press.

Galt, John,1984. *Ringan Gilhaize, or, The Covenanters*. Edinburgh: Scottish Academic Press.

Gilbert, Sandra M. and Gubar, Susan, 1979. *The Madwoman in the Attic: the Woman Writer and the Nineteenth-Century Literary Imagination*. New Haven, CT: Yale University Press.

Gooch, Steve, 2001. *Writing a Play*, 3rd edn. London: A. & C. Black.

Gottlieb, Robert and Kimball, Robert (eds), 2000. *Reading Lyrics*. New York: Pantheon Books.

Hartley, L.P., 1958. *The Go-Between*. London: Penguin.

Herman, Vimala, 1995. *Dramatic Discourse: Dialogue as Interaction in Plays*. London: Routledge.

Hirschkop, Ken, 1999. *Mikhail Bakhtin: An Aesthetic for Democracy*. Oxford: Oxford University Press.

Hogg, James, 1983. *The Private Memoirs and Confessions of a Justified Sinner*. London: Penguin.

Holland, Merlin, 2003. *Irish Peacock and Scarlet Marquis: the Real Trial of Oscar Wilde*. London: Fourth Estate.

Hume, David, 1976. *The Natural History of Religion and Dialogues concerning Natural Religion*, ed. A. Wayne Colver and John Valdimir Price. Oxford: Oxford University Press.

Joyce, James, 2000. *A Portait of the Artist as a Young Man*, ed. Jeri Johnson. Oxford: Oxford University Press.

Kakutani, Michiko, 2008. 'Review of Richard Price, *Lush Life*', *New York Times*, 4 March.

Kingman, John, 1988. *Report of the Committee of Inquiry into the Teaching of the English Language appointed by the Secretary of State under the Chairmanship of Sir John Kingman*. London: HMSO.

Kleist, Heinrich von, 1997. *Selected Writings*, ed. and tr. David Constantine. London: Dent.

Landor, Walter S., 1927. *The Complete Works of Walter Savage Landor*, ed. T. Earle. London: Welby, Chapman and Hall.

Leavis, F.R., 1948. *The Great Tradition*, London: Chatto and Windus.

——, 1952. 'Literature and Society' [first published 1943], in *The Common Pursuit*. London: Penguin, 182–94.

——, 1979. *Education and the University: A Sketch for an 'English School'*, 2nd edition [1st edition 1943]. Cambridge: Cambridge University Press.

Lentricchia, Frank, and McLaughlin, Thomas (eds), 1995. *Critical Terms for Literary Study*, 2nd edn. Chicago and London: University of Chicago Press.

Lodge, David, 1990. *After Bakhtin: Essays on Fiction and Criticism*. London: Routledge.

Lodge, David, and Wood, Nigel (eds), 2008. *Modern Criticism and Theory: A Reader*, 3rd edn [1st edition 1988]. London: Pearson.

Miller, Arthur, 1961. *A View from the Bridge and All My Sons*. London: Penguin.

Mittelstrass, Jürgen, 1988. 'On Socratic Dialogue', in *Platonic Writings – Platonic Readings*, ed. Charles L Griswold Jr. London: Routledge, 126–42.

Ohmann, Richard, 1973. 'Literature as Act'. In Seymour Chatman (ed.), *Approaches to Poetics*. New York: Columbia University Press, 81–107.

Pearce, Lynne, 1994. *Reading Dialogics*. London: Edward Arnold.

Pinter, Harold, 1965. *The Homecoming*. London: Methuen.

Plato, 1993. *Republic*, tr. Robin Waterfield. Oxford: Oxford University Press.

——, 1995. *Phaedrus*, tr Alexander Nehamas and Paul Woodruff. Indianapolis: Hackett Publishing.

Pulman, Philip. 2004. 'The Art of Reading in Colour'. *Index on Censorship*, vol 33, (October), 156–63.

Rushdie, Salman, 1988. *The Satanic Verses*. London: Viking.